The Entrepreneurs' Playbook

START YOUR BUSINESS TODAY

ROBERT HOPKINS

STRIVE's business playbook is a comprehensive document that outlines the strategies, processes, and procedures that a company follows to achieve its goals and objectives. It serves as a guide for employees and stakeholders, providing them with a clear understanding of how the business operates and what is expected of them.

STRIVE Coaching Inc.
https//:s-t-r-i-v-e.com

The Entreupreneur's Playbook

ISBN: [ISBN Number]

Copyright © 2024 by Robert Hopkins*

All rights reserved. No part of this book may be reproduced, stored in a retrieval system, or transmitted in any form or by any means, electronic, mechanical, photocopying, recording, or otherwise, without the prior written permission of the publisher.

Printed in USA
First Edition: June, 2024

Library of Congress Cataloging-in-Publication Data

For information about special discounts for bulk purchases, contact Robert Hopkins at STRIVE Coaching, Inc., https//:s-t-r-i-v-e.com.

Table of Contents

Introduction V

Chapter 1
Overview of the Company 1

Chapter 2
Creating your Company Identity and Logo 4
    2.1 Creating Your Business Mission, Vision and Principles   5
    2.2 Building out Your Story   7

Chapter 3
Organizational Structure 9
    3.1 Key Personnel and Roles   11
    3.2 Defining the Roles within the Company   13
    3.3 Business Strategy   14
    3.4 Market Analysis   16
    3.5 Competitive Landscape   18
    3.6 Value Proposition   20
    3.7 Strategic Goals and Initiatives   22

Chapter 4
Core Processes 25
    4.1 Sales and Marketing   28

Chapter 5
Operations and Production 31
    5.1 Finance and Accounting   33
    5.2 Human Resources   36
    5.3 Information Technology   38
    5.4 Customer Service   42

Chapter 6
Policies and Procedures 45
    6.1 Procedures   46
    6.2 Legal and Compliance Policies/ Compliance   48
    6.3 Financial Policies   50
    6.4 HR Policies   52

6.5	IT Policies Information Technology	55
6.6	Customer Service Policies	58
6.7	Key Performance Indicators (KPIs)	61
6.8	Measurement and Reporting Process	64
6.9	Targets and Benchmarks	66

Chapter 7
Technology and Tools Technology 69

7.1	Software and Systems Used	71
7.2	Training and Support Resources	74
7.3	Data Security Measures	76

Chapter 8
Training and Development. 80

8.1	Onboarding Process	82
8.2	Ongoing Training Programs	85
8.3	Career Development Opportunities	88

Chapter 9
Communication and Collaboration 92

9.1	Internal Communication Channels	94
9.2	Team Collaboration Tools	99
9.3	Meetings and Reporting Structure	101

Chapter 10
Crisis Management and Contingency Plans 105

10.1	Emergency Response Procedures	106
10.2	Business Continuity Planning	108

Chapter 11
Continuous Improvement 111

11.1	Feedback Mechanisms	113
11.2	Process Improvement Initiatives	115

Lessons Learned and Best Practices 118

Conclusion 121

Call to Action 124

Introduction

Welcome to STRIVE's Business Playbook — your comprehensive guide to navigating the complexities of our dynamic business environment and achieving unparalleled success. In this playbook, we have curated a collection of strategies, processes, and best practices that serve as the foundation for excellence in every aspect of our operations.

Importance of Using the Plays within the Playbook:

In today's fast-paced and ever-changing business landscape, having a playbook is not just advantageous; it's essential for staying ahead of the curve and driving sustainable growth. Here's why considering and utilizing the plays within our playbook are critical for our company's success:

Guidance Amid Uncertainty:

The business world is inherently unpredictable, with challenges and opportunities arising unexpectedly. By following the plays outlined in our playbook, we provide ourselves with a roadmap to navigate uncertainty, make informed decisions, and capitalize on opportunities as they arise.

Consistency and Standardization:

Consistency is key to building trust with customers, stakeholders, and partners. By adhering to the plays within our playbook, we ensure consistency in our processes, operations, and customer experiences, setting a high standard for quality and reliability.

Efficiency and Effectiveness:

This playbook is designed to optimize efficiency and effectiveness across all areas of our business. By utilizing the plays within the playbook, we streamline workflows, eliminate redundancies, and maximize productivity, enabling us to achieve more with less and drive greater results.

Continuous Improvement:

The plays within our playbook are not static; they evolve based on our experiences, insights, and lessons learned. By actively considering and implementing these plays, we demonstrate our commitment to continuous improvement, innovation, and learning, positioning ourselves for long-term success.

Alignment and Collaboration:

The playbook serves as a common reference point that aligns and unifies our team towards shared goals and objectives. By using the plays within the playbook, we foster collaboration, communication, and alignment across departments, functions, and levels of the organization, harnessing the collective wisdom and expertise of our team.

Risk Mitigation and Resilience:

In today's volatile business environment, risk mitigation is paramount. The plays within our playbook include strategies for identifying, assessing, and mitigating risks, ensuring that we are prepared to weather storms and emerge stronger and more resilient in the face of adversity.

Driving Innovation and Adaptation:

This playbook is not just about following established processes; it's also about fostering innovation, creativity, and adaptability. By encouraging the exploration and experimentation of new plays, we empower our team to innovate, adapt to changing market dynamics, and stay ahead of the competition.

In essence, the business playbook is more than just a document; it's a blueprint for success, a guidebook for excellence, and a roadmap to achieving our goals and aspirations. By considering and utilizing the plays within our playbook, we position ourselves for success in today's competitive business landscape and lay the foundation for a future filled with growth, prosperity, and lasting impact.

Chapter 1
Overview of the Company

Let's build out this playbook of the company by utilizing the following chapters and the contents herein will assist in developing

The overview of a company provides a concise summary of key information about the organization, its mission, vision, values, history, and core competencies. It serves as an introduction to the company and helps stakeholders, including investors, partners, customers, and employees, understand its identity, purpose, and strategic direction. Here's an outline of what an overview of a company typically includes:

Creating the Company's Identity

Company Name and Logo:
   Begin with the official name of the company and display its logo for visual identification.

Mission Statement:
   A brief statement that defines the company's purpose, why it exists, and the value it aims to deliver to its customers or stakeholders.

Vision Statement:
   An aspirational statement that describes the company's long term goals and desired future state.

Core Values:
   Key principles or beliefs that guide the company's actions and decisions. Core values reflect the company's culture and serve as a foundation for its behavior.

History and Background:
   Provide a brief overview of the company's founding, growth, and significant milestones. Highlight key achievements, awards, and recognitions.

Products or Services:

Describe the products or services offered by the company. Provide an overview of their features, benefits, and unique selling points.

Market Presence:

Outline the company's position in the market, including its target audience, industry sector, geographic reach, and competitive landscape.

Core Competencies:

Identify the company's key strengths, capabilities, and areas of expertise that set it apart from competitors.

Strategic Objectives:

Highlight the company's strategic goals and priorities for growth, expansion, innovation, or market leadership.

Financial Highlights:

Provide key financial metrics such as revenue, profitability, growth rate, and market share (if applicable).

Organizational Structure:

Describe the company's organizational hierarchy, including key leadership positions and reporting relationships.

Corporate Social Responsibility (CSR):

Discuss the company's commitment to social, environmental, and ethical responsibility, including any sustainability initiatives or community engagement efforts.

Awards and Accolades:

Highlight any industry awards, certifications, or recognition received by the company for its achievements or contributions.

Contact Information:

Include contact details such as the company's address, phone number, email, and website for further inquiries or collaboration opportunities.

Overall, an overview of a company provides a snapshot of its identity, history, capabilities, and aspirations, helping stakeholders gain a deeper understanding of what the company stands for and what it aims to achieve in the marketplace.

Consider testing multiple options through surveys, polls, or A/B testing to identify the most resonant choice.

Legal Considerations:

Conduct trademark searches to ensure the availability of the chosen name and logo and avoid potential legal disputes.

Consider consulting with legal professionals to secure trademark registration and protect intellectual property rights.

Scalability and Accessibility:

Ensure the name and logo are scalable and legible across different sizes and resolutions, from small digital icons to large format displays.

Prioritize accessibility by designing a logo that is easily recognizable and interpretable for individuals with disabilities.

Timelessness and Longevity:

Aim for a timeless design that will remain relevant and effective over the long term, avoiding trends or fads that may quickly become outdated.

Consider how the name and logo will resonate with future generations and withstand changes in consumer preferences or industry trends.

Emotional Appeal and Storytelling:

Infuse the name and logo with emotional appeal and storytelling elements that resonate with your target audience and evoke positive associations.

Communicate the brand's story, values, and unique selling proposition through the design and messaging of the logo.

By carefully considering these factors and conducting thorough research and analysis, you can select a compelling company name and design a memorable logo that effectively communicates your brand identity and resonates with your target audience.

Chapter 2
Creating your Company Identity and Logo

Choosing a company name and logo is a crucial decision for any business, as it represents the brand identity and plays a significant role in shaping public perception. Here are factors to consider when selecting a company name and designing a logo:

Relevance and Memorability:

Choose a name and logo that reflect the core values, mission, and offerings of your business.

Ensure the name is easy to remember, pronounce, and spell to facilitate brand recognition and recall.

Uniqueness and Differentiation:

Conduct thorough research to ensure the chosen name and logo are distinct from competitors and not infringing on existing trademarks

Aim for a unique and memorable design that stands out in the marketplace and captures the attention of your target audience.

Scalability and Flexibility:

Select a name and logo that can grow with your business and accommodate future expansions or diversifications.

Ensure the logo is versatile and adaptable across various mediums, including digital platforms, print materials, signage, and merchandise.

Consistency with Brand Identity:

Align the name and logo with your brand identity, including brand values, personality, tone, and visual aesthetics.

Ensure consistency between the name, logo, and other brand elements to convey a cohesive and unified brand image.

Market Research and Feedback:

Conduct market research and gather feedback from potential customers, stakeholders, and focus groups to assess the appeal and effectiveness of the name and logo.

Consider testing multiple options through surveys, polls, or A/B testing to identify the most resonant choice.

Legal Considerations:
Conduct trademark searches to ensure the availability of the chosen name and logo and avoid potential legal disputes.
Consider consulting with legal professionals to secure trademark registration and protect intellectual property rights.

Scalability and Accessibility:
Ensure the name and logo are scalable and legible across different sizes and resolutions, from small digital icons to large format displays
Prioritize accessibility by designing a logo that is easily recognizable and interpretable for individuals with disabilities.

Timelessness and Longevity:
Aim for a timeless design that will remain relevant and effective over the long term, avoiding trends or fads that may quickly become outdated.
Consider how the name and logo will resonate with future generations and withstand changes in consumer preferences or industry trends.

Emotional Appeal and Storytelling:
Infuse the name and logo with emotional appeal and storytelling elements that resonate with your target audience and evoke positive associations.
Communicate the brand's story, values, and unique selling proposition through the design and messaging of the logo.

By carefully considering these factors and conducting thorough research and analysis, you can select a compelling company name and design a memorable logo that effectively communicates your brand identity and resonates with your target audience.

Chapter 2.1

Creating Your Business Mission, Vision and Principles

In business, the terms "Mission," "Vision," and "Values" represent core elements of an organization's identity, purpose, and guiding principles. Here's what each of these concepts typically entails:

Mission:
The mission statement articulates the fundamental purpose or reason for existence of the organization. It answers the question, "What do we do?" and defines the primary objective or function that the company aims to fulfill.

A well crafted mission statement is clear, concise, and inspiring, capturing the essence of the organization's activities and its impact on stakeholders.

The mission statement serves as a guiding framework for decision-making, goal setting, and strategic direction within the organization.

Vision:
The vision statement describes the desired future state or long term aspiration that the organization seeks to achieve. It answers the question, "Where do we want to be?"

A compelling vision statement paints a vivid picture of what success looks like for the organization, inspiring employees, customers, and stakeholders to rally behind a shared vision of the future.

The vision statement provides direction and motivation, guiding the organization's strategic planning and goal-setting efforts as it works towards realizing its vision.

Values:
Values represent the core beliefs, principles, and ethical standards that guide the behavior and decision-making of individuals within the organization. They answer the question, "How do we conduct ourselves?"

Organizational values serve as a moral compass, influencing the culture, norms, and practices of the company. They define the behaviors and attitudes that are encouraged and rewarded, shaping the organization's identity and reputation.

Values alignment is important for fostering a positive work environment, building trust and cohesion among employees, and maintaining integrity and accountability throughout the organization.

In summary, the mission statement defines the organization's purpose, the vision statement outlines its future aspirations, and the values articulate the guiding principles that shape its culture and behavior. Together, these elements form the foundation of the organization's identity and provide a framework for decision-making, goal setting, and organizational alignment.

Chapter 2.2

Building out Your Story

History and Background

The history and background of a business provide a narrative overview of its origins, development, growth, key milestones, and significant events throughout its existence. It helps stakeholders understand the context and evolution of the company, its values, and its journey to its current state. Here's what the history and background of a business typically include:

Founding and Origins:

Describe the circumstances and motivations that led to the establishment of the business, including the founders' vision, goals, and initial aspirations.

Provide details about when and where the business was founded, by whom, and for what purpose.

Early Years and Growth:

Outline the early years of the business, including its initial operations, challenges, and achievements.

Highlight any significant milestones, breakthroughs, or innovations that contributed to the company's growth and success.

Key Milestones and Achievements:

Identify major milestones, achievements, and turning points in the company's history, such as product launches, expansions, acquisitions, or strategic partnerships.

Discuss how these milestones shaped the company's trajectory and contributed to its development and reputation.

Industry and Market Context:

Provide context about the industry or market in which the business operates, including trends, challenges, and competitive dynamics.

Discuss how the business has navigated industry changes and market trends over time.

Leadership and Management:

Highlight key leaders, executives, or influencers who have played significant roles in shaping the company's direction and culture.

Discuss the leadership style, values, and principles that have guided the company's management over the years.

Cultural and Organizational Aspects:

Describe the company's culture, values, and core beliefs, as well as any unique traditions or practices that define its identity.

Discuss how the company's culture has evolved and influenced its approach to business operations and employee relations.

Impact and Contributions:

Discuss the impact and contributions of the business to its industry, community, and society at large.

Highlight any philanthropic efforts, sustainability initiatives, or corporate social responsibility programs undertaken by the company.

Recent Developments and Future Outlook:

Provide an overview of recent developments, achievements, or changes within the company, including new product launches, expansions, or strategic shifts.

Discuss the company's future goals, aspirations, and strategies for continued growth and success.

The history and background of a business serve to provide stakeholders with a deeper understanding of the company's identity, values, and journey, fostering trust, loyalty, and engagement among employees, customers, investors, and partners.

Chapter 3
Organizational Structure

Organizational structure refers to the framework that outlines how an organization is designed, how authority is distributed, and how tasks are divided and coordinated. It defines the hierarchy, reporting relationships, and communication channels within the organization. Organizational structure can vary widely depending on factors such as the size of the organization, its industry, its culture, and its strategic objectives. Here are the key components and types of organizational structures commonly found in businesses:

Hierarchy:

Organizational hierarchy refers to the levels of authority and responsibility within the organization. It typically includes positions such as executives, managers, supervisors, and employees, arranged in a pyramidlike structure.

Chain of Command:

Chain of command defines the flow of authority and communication within the organization. It establishes who reports to whom and who has the authority to make decisions and issue directives.

Span of Control:

Span of control refers to the number of subordinates that a manager or supervisor is responsible for overseeing. A wider span of control means that a manager supervises more employees, while a narrower span of control means fewer direct reports.

Centralization vs. Decentralization:

Centralization refers to the concentration of decision-making authority at the top levels of the organization, while decentralization involves delegating decision-making authority to lower levels of the organization.

In centralized organizations, decisions are made by top management, while in decentralized organizations, decisions are delegated to managers and employees at lower levels.

Functional Structure:

In a functional organizational structure, employees are grouped based on their specialized functions or areas of expertise, such as marketing, finance, operations, or human resources.

Each department or function is led by a manager who oversees the activities and performance of employees within that area.

Divisional Structure:

A divisional organizational structure divides the organization into separate divisions or business units based on products, services, geographic regions, or customer segments.

Each division operates as a self contained entity with its own functions, resources, and decision-making authority.

Matrix Structure:

A matrix organizational structure combines elements of both functional and divisional structures, allowing employees to report to multiple managers or work across different departments or projects.

Employees may belong to both a functional department and a project team, resulting in dual reporting relationships.

Flat Structure:

A flat organizational structure has few or no levels of middle management between top management and frontline employees.

It promotes open communication, faster decision-making, and greater autonomy for employees, but may also lead to challenges in coordination and supervision.

Virtual Structure:

A virtual organizational structure consists of a network of independent contractors, remote workers, and outsourced partners who collaborate virtually to achieve common goals.

It relies heavily on technology and digital platforms to facilitate communication, collaboration, and coordination.

Hybrid Structure:

A hybrid organizational structure combines elements of different structures to suit the unique needs and objectives of the organization.

It may involve a mix of functional, divisional, and matrix structures, or incorporate aspects of both centralized and decentralized decision-making.

Organizational structure plays a critical role in shaping the culture, communication, and efficiency of an organization. The choice of structure depends on various factors, including the organization's size, industry, goals, and external environment. It's important for businesses to periodically review and adapt their organizational structure to ensure alignment with their strategic objectives and changing needs.

Chapter 3.1
Key Personnel and Roles

Key personnel and roles in a business refer to individuals who hold positions of significant responsibility and authority within the organization. These individuals play critical roles in driving the organization's strategic direction, managing operations, and achieving its goals. Here are some key personnel and their roles commonly found in businesses:

Chief Executive Officer (CEO):

The CEO is the highest ranking executive in the organization and is responsible for setting the overall strategic direction and vision for the company. They oversee the execution of business plans, manage relationships with stakeholders, and ensure the organization's longterm success.

Chief Operating Officer (COO):

The COO is responsible for overseeing the day-to-day operations of the company. They develop and implement operational strategies, manage business processes, and drive efficiency and productivity across the organization.

Chief Financial Officer (CFO):

The CFO is responsible for managing the company's financial operations and ensuring its financial health. They oversee financial planning, budgeting, accounting, and reporting, as well as financial risk management and capital allocation.

Chief Marketing Officer (CMO):

The CMO is responsible for developing and implementing marketing strategies to promote the company's products or services, generate leads, and build brand awareness. They oversee marketing campaigns, market research, branding, and customer acquisition efforts.

Chief Technology Officer (CTO):

The CTO is responsible for overseeing the organization's technology strategy and infrastructure. They lead technology initiatives, evaluate and implement new technologies, and ensure that the company's IT systems are secure, reliable, and aligned with business objectives.

Chief Human Resources Officer (CHRO):

The CHRO is responsible for managing the organization's human capital and talent management strategies. They oversee recruitment, training and development, compensation and benefits, employee relations, and organizational culture initiatives.

Chief Legal Officer (CLO) or General Counsel:

The CLO or General Counsel is responsible for providing legal counsel and guidance to the organization. They oversee legal compliance, risk management, contract negotiations, and litigation matters, ensuring that the company operates within the bounds of the law.

Vice Presidents and Directors:

Vice Presidents (VPs) and Directors typically oversee specific functional areas or departments within the organization, such as sales, operations, finance, marketing, or human resources. They are responsible for managing teams, setting goals, and driving performance in their respective areas.

Managers and Supervisors:

Managers and Supervisors are responsible for overseeing the day-to-day activities of teams or departments within the organization. They provide leadership, guidance, and support to employees, ensure that work is completed on time and within budget, and communicate organizational goals and expectations.

Individual Contributors:

Individual Contributors are employees who are responsible for carrying out specific tasks or responsibilities within their areas of expertise. They contribute to the achievement of organizational goals through their work and collaboration with colleagues.

These are just some of the key personnel and roles commonly found in businesses. The specific titles and responsibilities may vary depending on the size, industry, and structure of the organization.

Chapter 3.2

Defining the Roles within the Company

Defining Roles and responsibilities for key personnel Defining roles and responsibilities for a business involves clearly outlining the tasks, duties, and expectations associated with each position within the organization. This process helps ensure that employees understand their roles, know what is expected of them, and can effectively contribute to the achievement of organizational goals. Here's how to define roles and responsibilities for business:

Identify Key Functions and Positions:

Start by identifying the key functions and positions within the organization. Determine which roles are essential for achieving the company's objectives and supporting its operations.

Develop Job Descriptions:

Create detailed job descriptions for each position, outlining the responsibilities, duties, qualifications, and expectations associated with the role.

Specify the key tasks, activities, and deliverables that the employee will be responsible for, as well as any required skills, experience, or qualifications.

Clarify Reporting Relationships:

Define the reporting relationships within the organization by specifying who each employee reports to and who they are responsible for supervising or collaborating with.

Establish clear lines of communication and accountability to ensure that employees know who to go to for guidance, support, and deciion-making authority.

Set Expectations and Goals:

Clearly communicate performance expectations and goals for each role, including both quantitative and qualitative metrics for assessing performance.

Align individual goals with departmental and organizational objectives to ensure that everyone is working towards common goals and priorities.

Establish Role Boundaries and Authority:

Define the scope of each role by clarifying the boundaries of authority, decision-making autonomy, and areas of responsibility.

Specify any limitations or constraints that apply to the role, as well as any expectations for collaboration or coordination with other team members or departments.

Provide Training and Support:

Ensure that employees have the knowledge, skills, and resources they need to perform their roles effectively. Provide training, mentorship, and ongoing support as needed.

Encourage continuous learning and professional development to help employees grow and adapt to changing job requirements.

Document Roles and Responsibilities:

Document the defined roles and responsibilities in writing, such as in job descriptions, organizational charts, or employee handbooks.

Make this information easily accessible to employees so they can refer to it as needed and have a clear understanding of their role within the organization.

Regularly Review and Update:

Periodically review and update roles and responsibilities as needed to reflect changes in the business environment, organizational priorities, or individual performance.

Solicit feedback from employees, managers, and stakeholders to identify areas for improvement and ensure that roles remain relevant and aligned with organizational goals.

By defining roles and responsibilities clearly and comprehensively, businesses can promote clarity, accountability, and efficiency within the organization, leading to improved performance and outcomes.

Chapter 3.3

Business Strategy

Business strategy refers to a set of long term plans and actions designed to achieve specific goals and objectives that contribute to the overall success and sustainability of a business. A well defined business strategy outlines how the company will compete in its industry, create value for its customers, and achieve a competitive advantage. Here are key components of a business strategy:

Mission, Vision, and Values:

The mission statement defines the purpose and reason for the existence of the business, while the vision statement outlines its long term aspirations. Values represent the core principles and beliefs that guide the organization's behavior and decision-making.

Market Analysis:

Conduct a thorough analysis of the external environment, including market trends, customer needs, competitor actions, and industry dynamics. Identify opportunities and threats that may impact the business.

Competitive Positioning:

Determine how the business will differentiate itself from competitors and create value for its target customers. Define the company's unique selling proposition (USP) and competitive advantages.

Target Market and Segmentation:

Identify the target market segments that the business will focus on serving. Segment customers based on demographic, geographic, psychographic, or behavioral factors, and tailor products or services to meet their specific needs.

Product and Service Strategy:

Develop a product or service strategy that aligns with the needs and preferences of the target market. Define the product or service offerings, features, pricing, and positioning in the market.

Marketing and Sales Strategy:

Outline the marketing and sales tactics that will be used to attract, acquire, and retain customers. Develop strategies for brand building, lead generation, customer acquisition, and customer relationship management.

Operations Strategy:

Define the operational processes, systems, and resources required to deliver products or services efficiently and effectively. Consider factors such as production methods, supply chain management, quality control, and resource allocation.

Financial Strategy:

Develop a financial strategy that supports the achievement of business goals and objectives. This may include financial planning, budgeting, forecasting, capital allocation, and risk management.

Technology and Innovation Strategy:

Identify how technology and innovation will be leveraged to drive growth, improve efficiency, and enhance the customer experience. Develop strategies for adopting new technologies, investing in research and development, and fostering a culture of innovation.

Organizational Structure and Culture:

Define the organizational structure, roles, and responsibilities that support the execution of the business strategy. Cultivate a supportive and aligned organizational culture that encourages collaboration, innovation, and performance excellence.

Measurement and Evaluation:

Establish key performance indicators (KPIs) and metrics to track progress towards strategic goals and objectives. Regularly monitor and evaluate performance, and make adjustments to the strategy as needed.

Risk Management and Contingency Planning:

Identify potential risks and uncertainties that may impact the business strategy, and develop strategies to mitigate and manage these risks. Implement contingency plans to address unforeseen events and disruptions.

By developing and implementing a comprehensive business strategy, organizations can enhance their competitiveness, drive growth and profitability, and achieve sustainable success in the marketplace.

Chapter 3.4

Market Analysis

Market analysis for business involves assessing various aspects of the market in which a company operates or intends to enter. It provides insights into the dynamics, trends, opportunities, and challenges within the market, helping businesses make informed decisions and develop effective strategies. Here are the key factors to include in a market analysis:

Market Size and Growth:

Determine the total size of the market in terms of revenue, units sold, or other relevant metrics. Analyze historical growth trends and forecast future growth potential.

Market Segmentation:

Divide the market into distinct segments based on factors such as demographics, geographic location, psychographics, behavior, or needs. Identify the most attractive target segments for the business.

Market Trends:

Identify current and emerging trends that are shaping the market, such as technological advancements, regulatory changes, shifts in consumer preferences, or changes in industry practices.

Market Drivers and Challenges:

Analyze the key drivers that are fueling growth and demand in the market, as well as the challenges or barriers that may hinder market expansion or profitability.

Competitive Landscape:

Assess the competitive environment within the market, including the number and strength of competitors, their market share, pricing strategies, product offerings, and competitive advantages.

SWOT Analysis:

Conduct a SWOT analysis to identify the strengths, weaknesses, opportunities, and threats facing the business within the market. This helps to understand the internal and external factors that may impact the company's performance.

Customer Analysis:

Understand the characteristics, preferences, needs, and behaviors of the target customers within the market. Identify customer segments, personas, and buying behaviors to tailor products, services, and marketing efforts accordingly.

Market Entry Barriers:

Identify any barriers to entry that may limit or impede new competitors from entering the market. This may include factors such as high capital requirements, regulatory restrictions, or strong incumbent competitors.

Distribution Channels:

Analyze the distribution channels through which products or services reach customers in the market. Evaluate the effectiveness of existing channels and identify opportunities for expansion or optimization.

Regulatory Environment:

Assess the regulatory landscape governing the market, including industry regulations, standards, certifications, and compliance requirements. Understand how regulatory changes may impact business operations and market dynamics.

Economic Factors:

Consider macroeconomic factors such as GDP growth, inflation rates, interest rates, and unemployment levels that may influence consumer spending patterns, market demand, and overall business performance.

Technology and Innovation:

Evaluate the role of technology and innovation within the market, including emerging technologies, disruptive trends, and opportunities for differentiation through innovation.

By conducting a comprehensive market analysis, businesses can gain valuable insights into the market landscape, identify growth opportunities, assess competitive threats, and make informed decisions to effectively position themselves for success.

Chapter 3.5
Competitive Landscape

The competitive landscape for business refers to the overall structure and dynamics of competition within a particular industry or market. It involves analyzing the various factors that influence competition among companies, including their strengths, weaknesses, strategies, and market positions. Here are the key factors to consider when assessing the competitive landscape:

Competitors:
Identify the companies that compete directly or indirectly with your business. Consider both traditional competitors (those offering similar products or services) and potential disruptors (new entrants or alternative solutions).

Market Share:
Determine the market share held by each competitor within the industry. This helps gauge their relative size and importance in the market.

Product or Service Offerings:
Analyze the range, quality, and differentiation of products or services offered by competitors. Assess how their offerings compare to yours in terms of features, pricing, and value proposition.

Strengths and Weaknesses:
Evaluate the strengths and weaknesses of each competitor, including their brand reputation, financial resources, technological capabilities, distribution networks, and customer loyalty.

Market Positioning:
Understand how competitors position themselves in the market relative to each other and to your own business. Identify their target customer segments, value propositions, and competitive advantages.

Pricing Strategy:
Analyze competitors' pricing strategies, including pricing levels, discounting practices, and promotional offers. Assess how their pricing decisions impact market dynamics and customer perceptions.

Marketing and Branding:
Assess competitors' marketing tactics, branding efforts, and customer engagement strategies. Evaluate the effectiveness of their advertising campaigns, social media presence, and customer loyalty programs.

Distribution Channels:
Understand how competitors distribute their products or services to customers. Analyze their distribution channels, partnerships, and logistics capabilities.

Customer Base:
Identify the types of customers that competitors target and serve.

Analyze their customer demographics, preferences, and purchasing behavior.

Innovation and R&D:

Evaluate competitors' investment in research and development (R&D) and their ability to innovate. Assess their track record of introducing new products, services, or technologies to the market.

Regulatory and Legal Factors:

Consider any regulatory or legal factors that may impact competition within the industry, such as industry regulations, intellectual property rights, or antitrust laws.

International Competition:

Assess competition from international companies that may operate in the same market or provide similar products or services globally.

By thoroughly analyzing the competitive landscape, businesses can gain valuable insights into their position within the market, identify opportunities for differentiation and growth, and develop effective strategies to compete more successfully.

Chapter 3.6

Value Proposition

A value proposition is a statement that summarizes the unique benefits and value that a company offers to its customers. It explains why customers should choose a particular product or service over alternatives available in the market. A strong value proposition communicates the distinctive advantages and solves specific pain points or needs of the target audience. Here are the key factors to consider when developing a value proposition for business:

Customer Needs and Pain Points:

Understand the needs, preferences, and pain points of your target customers. Identify the problems or challenges they face that your product or service can address.

Product or Service Benefits:

Clearly articulate the key benefits and outcomes that customers can expect from using your product or service. Highlight how your offering solves their problems, fulfills their desires, or improves their lives.

Points of Differentiation:

Identify what sets your product or service apart from competitors. Highlight unique features, capabilities, or qualities that differentiate your offering and create value for customers.

USP (Unique Selling Proposition):

Define your unique selling proposition or USP, which is the specific aspect of your product or service that makes it stand out in the market. This could be based on factors such as quality, price, innovation, convenience, or customer service.

Target Audience:

Tailor your value proposition to resonate with your target audience. Consider factors such as demographics, psychographics, behavior, and preferences when crafting your messaging.

Clarity and Simplicity:

Ensure that your value proposition is clear, concise, and easy to understand. Avoid jargon or technical language that may confuse or overwhelm customers.

Relevance and Context:

Make sure your value proposition is relevant to the needs and interests of your target customers. Position your offering in a way that resonates with their specific context, situation, or motivations.

Credibility and Trustworthiness:

Build credibility and trust by providing evidence or proof to support your value proposition. This could include customer testimonials, case studies, certifications, awards, or guarantees.

Emotional Appeal:

Appeal to the emotions and aspirations of your target audience. Communicate how your product or service can make them feel, whether it's happy, confident, successful, or secure.

Consistency Across Touchpoints:

Ensure consistency in your value proposition across all customer touchpoints, including your website, marketing materials, advertising campaigns, and sales interactions.

Adaptability and Flexibility:

Be prepared to adapt and evolve your value proposition over time in response to changes in the market, customer feedback, or competitive dynamics.

Measurable Outcomes:
Communicate the specific outcomes or benefits that customers can expect from using your product or service. This could include quantifiable results such as cost savings, increased efficiency, improved performance, or enhanced satisfaction.

By considering these factors and crafting a compelling value proposition, businesses can effectively communicate the unique benefits and advantages of their offerings, attract customers, and differentiate themselves in the market.

Chapter 3.7
Strategic Goals and Initiatives

Strategic goals and initiatives are key components of a business's strategic planning process. Strategic goals represent the overarching objectives that a company aims to achieve to fulfill its mission and vision, while initiatives are specific actions or projects designed to support the attainment of those goals. Here are the factors to consider when developing strategic goals and initiatives for business:

Alignment with Mission and Vision:
Ensure that strategic goals and initiatives are aligned with the company's mission, vision, and core values. They should reflect the overarching purpose and long term aspirations of the organization.

SMART Criteria:
Make strategic goals Specific, Measurable, Achievable, Relevant, and Timebound (SMART). This ensures clarity, accountability, and effectiveness in goal setting.

Priority and Focus:
Prioritize strategic goals based on their importance and impact on the business's success. Focus on a few key goals that are most critical to achieving the desired outcomes.

Market Analysis:
Conduct a thorough analysis of the external market environment to identify opportunities, threats, and trends that may impact strategic goals. Consider factors such as market dynamics, customer needs, competitor actions, and regulatory changes.

Internal Capabilities and Resources:
Assess the organization's internal strengths, weaknesses, capabilities, and resources to determine its ability to achieve strategic goals. Identify any gaps or constraints that need to be addressed to support successful implementation.

Risk Assessment:
Identify potential risks and uncertainties that may affect the achievement of strategic goals. Develop risk mitigation strategies and contingency plans to address these challenges.

Stakeholder Engagement:
Involve key stakeholders, including employees, customers, suppliers, investors, and partners, in the strategic planning process. Seek input, feedback, and buy in to ensure alignment and support for strategic goals and initiatives.

Long Term and Short Term Objectives:
Define both long term strategic goals that provide direction and vision for the organization and short term objectives that drive action and progress towards those goals. Break down long term goals into smaller, achievable milestones.

Resource Allocation:
Allocate resources, including financial, human, and technological resources, effectively to support the implementation of strategic initiatives. Ensure that resources are aligned with strategic priorities and allocated based on their impact and importance.

Measurement and Tracking:
Establish key performance indicators (KPIs) and metrics to measure progress towards strategic goals. Develop a monitoring and evaluation framework to track performance, identify areas of improvement, and make data driven decisions.

Flexibility and Adaptability:
Maintain flexibility and adaptability in strategic planning to

respond to changing market conditions, emerging opportunities, or unexpected challenges. Be willing to adjust goals and initiatives as needed to stay competitive and achieve success.

Communication and Transparency:

Communicate strategic goals and initiatives clearly and consistently to all stakeholders within the organization. Foster transparency and open communication to ensure understanding, alignment, and commitment to the strategic plan.

By considering these factors and developing strategic goals and initiatives that are well defined, focused, and aligned with the organization's mission and capabilities, businesses can increase their chances of success and drive sustainable growth in the long term.

Chapter 4

Core Processes

Core processes are the fundamental activities or workflows that are essential for the functioning of a business. They represent the primary functions and operations that enable the organization to deliver value to its customers, achieve its strategic objectives, and sustain its operations. While specific core processes may vary depending on the nature of the business, industry, and size of the organization, there are several common core processes that are integral to most businesses:

Product Development or Service Design:

This process involves the conception, design, development, and testing of products or services. It includes activities such as market research, ideation, prototyping, engineering, and quality assurance.

Marketing and Sales:

The marketing and sales process encompasses activities related to attracting, engaging, and converting customers. It includes market segmentation, advertising, lead generation, sales prospecting, customer relationship management, and closing deals.

Operations Management:

Operations management involves the efficient and effective management of resources, processes, and activities to produce goods or deliver services. It includes production planning, inventory management, supply chain logistics, quality control, and process optimization.

Customer Service and Support:

Customer service and support processes focus on providing assistance, resolving inquiries, and addressing customer needs and concerns. It includes activities such as handling inquiries, providing technical support, managing complaints, and ensuring customer satisfaction.

Financial Management:

Financial management processes involve the management of

financial resources, budgeting, accounting, and financial reporting. It includes activities such as budget planning, financial analysis, cash flow management, and financial risk management.

In the areas of financial management there are a myriad of proceeses or systems that should be considered . These systems that should be considered are

For a business in the area of finance and accounting, several key processes should be included to ensure effective financial management and compliance. Here are some essential processes:

1. Budgeting and Forecasting: Developing budgets and financial forecasts to plan and allocate resources effectively.
2. Financial Reporting: Generating accurate and timely financial statements such as balance sheets, income statements, and cash flow statements for internal and external stakeholders.
3. Accounts Payable: Managing invoices and payments to suppliers and vendors in a timely manner to maintain good relationships and avoid late fees.
4. Accounts Receivable: Tracking customer invoices, following up on overdue payments, and managing credit policies to optimize cash flow.
5. Payroll Processing: Calculating and disbursing employee salaries, benefits, and taxes accurately and on time.
6. Tax Compliance: Ensuring compliance with relevant tax laws and regulations, including filing tax returns, remitting taxes, and handling tax audits.
7. Financial Analysis: Analyzing financial data to assess performance, identify trends, and make informed decisions about resource allocation and strategic planning.
8. Internal Controls: Establishing and maintaining internal controls to safeguard assets, prevent fraud, and ensure the accuracy of financial reporting.
9. Risk Management: Identifying, assessing, and mitigating financial risks such as market risk, credit risk, and operational risk.
10. Audit Preparation: Preparing for internal and external audits by organizing financial records, documenting procedures, and addressing any audit findings.
11. Cash Management: Monitoring cash flow, optimizing working capital, and managing liquidity to meet financial obligations and maximize profitability.

12. Compliance and Regulatory Reporting: Ensuring compliance with relevant laws, regulations, and accounting standards, and preparing necessary regulatory filings.
13. Financial Planning and Analysis (FP&A): Collaborating with business units to develop financial plans, analyze performance against targets, and support strategic decision-making.
14. Capital Budgeting: Evaluating investment opportunities, allocating capital resources, and assessing the financial feasibility of projects or acquisitions.
15. Financial Systems Management: Implementing and maintaining financial software systems to streamline processes, improve data accuracy, and enhance reporting capabilities.

By incorporating these processes into their operations, businesses can effectively manage their finances, optimize performance, and mitigate risks in the dynamic business environment.

Human Resources Management:

Human resources management encompasses activities related to recruiting, hiring, training, managing, and developing employees. It includes functions such as workforce planning, performance management, employee relations, and talent development.

Information Technology (IT) Management:

IT management processes involve the planning, implementation, and maintenance of information technology systems and infrastructure. It includes activities such as IT strategy development, system deployment, network management, cybersecurity, and data management.

Strategic Planning and Management:

Strategic planning and management processes focus on defining the organization's vision, mission, goals, and strategies for achieving long term success. It includes activities such as strategic analysis, goal setting, strategy formulation, implementation planning, and performance monitoring.

Quality Management:

Quality management processes aim to ensure that products or services meet or exceed customer expectations and quality standards. It includes activities such as quality planning, quality assurance, quality control, and continuous improvement.

Risk Management:

Risk management processes involve identifying, assessing, mitigating, and monitoring risks that may impact the organization's objectives and operations. It includes activities such as risk identification, risk analysis, risk treatment, and risk monitoring.

These core processes form the foundation of a business's operations and are essential for its success and sustainability. Effective management and optimization of these processes are critical for achieving operational excellence, delivering value to customers, and maintaining a competitive advantage in the marketplace.

Chapter 4.1

Sales and Marketing

Sales and marketing are two closely related functions within a business that work together to attract, engage, and convert customers. While they serve distinct purposes, they both play crucial roles in driving revenue and growth. Here's an overview of sales and marketing, along with key factors to consider for business:

Sales:

Sales involve the process of directly engaging with prospects or customers to generate revenue through the sale of products or services. It focuses on building relationships, understanding customer needs, and closing deals. Key activities in sales include prospecting, lead qualification, product demonstrations, negotiations, and closing sales.

Marketing:

Marketing encompasses a broader set of activities aimed at promoting products or services, building brand awareness, and generating demand among target audiences. It involves understanding customer needs and preferences, creating compelling messaging and content, and delivering it through various channels to attract and engage prospects. Key marketing activities include market research, branding, advertising, content creation, social media marketing, email marketing, and public relations.

Factors to Consider for Business in Sales and Marketing:

Target Audience:

Identify and understand the characteristics, preferences, and behaviors of your target audience. Develop detailed buyer personas to tailor sales and marketing efforts to their specific needs and interests.

Market Analysis:

Conduct market research to assess the competitive landscape, identify market trends, and understand customer needs and preferences. Use this information to inform sales and marketing strategies and tactics.

Value Proposition:

Clearly articulate the unique value proposition of your products or services and communicate it effectively to your target audience. Highlight the benefits and advantages that set your offerings apart from competitors.

Branding and Positioning:

Develop a strong brand identity and positioning that resonates with your target audience. Ensure consistency in branding across all marketing channels and touchpoints to build brand recognition and trust.

Sales Process:

Define a clear sales process that outlines the steps from lead generation to closing deals. Train sales representatives on effective selling techniques, objection handling, and relationship building to maximize sales effectiveness.

Marketing Strategy:

Develop a comprehensive marketing strategy that encompasses various channels and tactics to reach and engage your target audience. Consider a mix of online and offline channels, including digital marketing, social media, content marketing, email marketing, events, and traditional advertising.

Lead Generation and Nurturing:

Implement strategies for lead generation to attract potential customers and convert them into qualified leads. Develop lead nurturing campaigns to build relationships with prospects and guide them through the sales funnel.

Customer Relationship Management (CRM):

Use CRM systems to track and manage customer interactions, sales activities, and pipeline management. Leverage customer data to personalize communication and improve sales and marketing effectiveness.

Metrics and Analytics:

Monitor and measure key performance indicators (KPIs) to evaluate the effectiveness of sales and marketing efforts. Analyze metrics such as lead conversion rates, customer acquisition costs, customer lifetime value, and return on investment (ROI) to optimize strategies and tactics.

Continuous Improvement:

Regularly review and refine sales and marketing strategies based on feedback, performance data, and market changes. Experiment with new approaches, technologies, and channels to stay competitive and drive continuous improvement.

By considering these factors and effectively aligning sales and marketing efforts, businesses can attract, engage, and convert customers more effectively, drive revenue growth, and build long term relationships with their target audience.

Chapter 5

Operations and Production

Operations and production are essential functions within a business responsible for managing the processes and activities involved in producing goods or delivering services. While operations focus on the overall management of resources and processes to ensure efficiency and effectiveness, production specifically refers to the processes involved in manufacturing or creating products. Here's a closer look at operations and production in business:

Operations:

Operations management involves overseeing the day-to-day activities and processes that are necessary for the business to function smoothly and efficiently. This includes managing resources, optimizing processes, and ensuring that business operations align with strategic objectives. Key aspects of operations management include:

Resource Management:

Managing resources such as human capital, equipment, materials, and facilities to ensure optimal utilization and efficiency.

Factors to Consider while Building out this Play

Process Optimization:

Streamlining and improving processes to enhance productivity, reduce costs, and deliver higher quality products or services.

Supply Chain Management:

Managing the flow of materials, information, and finances across the supply chain, from suppliers to customers, to ensure timely delivery and minimize disruptions.

Quality Control:

Implementing measures to monitor and maintain product or service quality, identify defects or issues, and continuously improve processes.

Inventory Management:

Managing inventory levels to ensure sufficient stock is available to meet demand while minimizing excess inventory and associated costs.

Capacity Planning:

Forecasting demand and adjusting production capacity to meet customer needs efficiently without over or underutilizing resources.

Logistics and Distribution:

Managing the movement and storage of goods, including transportation, warehousing, and distribution, to ensure timely delivery to customers.

Risk Management:

Identifying potential risks and implementing strategies to mitigate or manage risks that may impact operations, such as supply chain disruptions, regulatory changes, or natural disasters.

Production:

Production refers to the processes involved in manufacturing or creating goods or services. It encompasses the transformation of raw materials or inputs into finished products through a series of operations and activities. Key aspects of production management include:

Manufacturing Processes:

Planning and executing manufacturing processes, including machining, assembly, fabrication, or chemical processing, depending on the nature of the product.

Workforce Management:

Managing production teams and personnel to ensure that they are properly trained, motivated, and equipped to perform their roles effectively.

Production Planning and Scheduling:

Developing production plans and schedules to optimize resource utilization, minimize bottlenecks, and meet customer demand efficiently.

Quality Assurance:

Implementing quality control measures to ensure that products meet specified quality standards and regulatory requirements.

Maintenance and Reliability:

Ensuring that production equipment and machinery are properly maintained and reliable to minimize downtime and maximize productivity.

Lean Manufacturing:
Implementing lean principles and practices to eliminate waste, improve efficiency, and enhance value delivery throughout the production process.

Continuous Improvement:
Encouraging a culture of continuous improvement to identify opportunities for efficiency gains, cost reduction, and quality enhancement in production operations.

Safety and Compliance:
Ensuring compliance with safety regulations and standards to protect workers and prevent accidents or injuries in the production environment.

Overall, operations and production are critical functions within a business that work together to ensure the efficient and effective delivery of goods or services to customers. By effectively managing operations and production processes, businesses can enhance competitiveness, improve customer satisfaction, and achieve sustainable growth.

Chapter 5.1

Finance and Accounting

Finance and accounting are two interconnected functions within a business that are essential for managing financial resources, tracking financial performance, and ensuring compliance with regulatory requirements. While finance focuses on the broader management of financial resources and strategic decision-making, accounting involves the recording, analysis, and reporting of financial transactions. Here's a closer look at finance and accounting in business:

Finance:
Finance is the function responsible for managing the financial resources of the business and making strategic decisions to maximize shareholder value. It involves assessing investment opportunities,

securing funding, managing risks, and optimizing financial performance. Key aspects of finance include:

Capital Budgeting:

Evaluating investment opportunities and allocating capital to projects or initiatives that generate the highest return on investment.

Financial Planning and Analysis:

Developing financial forecasts, budgets, and strategic plans to guide decision-making and resource allocation.

Risk Management:

Identifying and assessing financial risks, such as market risk, credit risk, and operational risk, and implementing strategies to mitigate or manage these risks.

Corporate Finance:

Managing capital structure, including debt and equity financing, and making decisions related to dividends, stock repurchases, and mergers and acquisitions.

Financial Reporting:

Communicating financial performance and results to stakeholders through financial statements, reports, and presentations, in compliance with accounting standards and regulatory requirements.

Treasury Management:

Managing cash flow, liquidity, and short term investments to ensure sufficient funds are available to meet operational needs and financial obligations.

Financial Compliance:

Ensuring compliance with financial regulations, laws, and standards, such as Generally Accepted Accounting Principles (GAAP) or International Financial Reporting Standards (IFRS).

Financial Strategy:

Developing and implementing strategies to optimize financial performance, enhance shareholder value, and achieve long term sustainability and growth.

Accounting:

Accounting is the process of recording, analyzing, and reporting financial transactions and information related to the business. It provides valuable insights into the financial health and performance of the organization, facilitating decision-making and accountability. Key aspects of accounting include:

Bookkeeping:

Recording financial transactions, such as sales, purchases, expenses, and revenues, in accounting journals or ledgers.

Financial Reporting:

Preparing financial statements, including the balance sheet, income statement, cash flow statement, and statement of retained earnings, to communicate the financial position and performance of the business.

Auditing:

Conducting internal or external audits to review financial records, assess compliance with accounting standards and regulations, and provide assurance on the accuracy and reliability of financial reporting.

Tax Accounting:

Calculating and reporting taxes owed to governmental authorities, including income taxes, sales taxes, and payroll taxes, and ensuring compliance with tax laws and regulations.

Cost Accounting:

Analyzing and allocating costs to products, services, or activities to assess profitability, support pricing decisions, and control costs.

Managerial Accounting:

Providing internal financial information and analysis to support managerial decision-making, such as budgeting, cost control, performance evaluation, and strategic planning.

Forensic Accounting:

Investigating financial fraud, misconduct, or irregularities by analyzing financial records, tracing transactions, and providing expert testimony in legal proceedings.

Finance and accounting work together to ensure the effective management of financial resources, accurate financial reporting, and compliance with regulatory requirements. By maintaining sound financial management practices and leveraging financial data and analysis, businesses can make informed decisions, allocate resources efficiently, and achieve their strategic objectives.

Chapter 5.2

Human Resources

Human resources (HR) is a critical function within a business responsible for managing the organization's most valuable asset: its people. HR is tasked with attracting, developing, and retaining talent, as well as creating a positive work environment conducive to employee productivity and satisfaction. Here's an overview of HR and the key factors to consider for business:

Recruitment and Hiring:

HR oversees the recruitment and hiring process, from identifying staffing needs to sourcing candidates, screening resumes, conducting interviews, and extending job offers. Factors to consider include:
- Defining job roles and responsibilities
- Developing job descriptions and qualifications
- Utilizing effective recruitment channels
- Ensuring a fair and unbiased selection process

Employee Onboarding:

HR facilitates the onboarding process for new hires, providing them with the information, resources, and training they need to acclimate to their roles and the organization. Factors to consider include:
- Developing onboarding programs and materials
- Providing training and orientation sessions
- Assigning mentors or buddy systems for support
- Soliciting feedback to improve the onboarding experience

Employee Relations:

HR manages employee relations and handles issues or conflicts that may arise in the workplace. This includes addressing grievances, resolving disputes, and fostering positive relationships among employees. Factors to consider include:
- Establishing open communication channels
- Implementing conflict resolution strategies
- Enforcing company policies and procedures
- Promoting a culture of respect and collaboration

Performance Management:

HR oversees performance management processes to assess and

enhance employee performance, productivity, and development. This includes setting goals, conducting performance evaluations, providing feedback, and identifying areas for improvement. Factors to consider include:
- Establishing clear performance expectations
- Providing regular feedback and coaching
- Recognizing and rewarding achievements
- Offering opportunities for skill development and growth

Training and Development:

HR coordinates training and development initiatives to enhance employee skills, knowledge, and capabilities. This may involve offering workshops, seminars, online courses, and other learning opportunities to support career advancement and professional growth. Factors to consider include:
- Assessing training needs and priorities
- Developing training programs and materials
- Providing access to learning resources and tools
- Evaluating the effectiveness of training initiatives

Compensation and Benefits:

HR manages compensation and benefits programs to attract, motivate, and retain employees. This includes setting competitive salary structures, administering employee benefits such as healthcare and retirement plans, and ensuring compliance with compensation laws and regulations. Factors to consider include:
- Benchmarking salaries and benefits against industry standards
- Designing incentive programs to reward performance
- Communicating compensation and benefits information to employees
- Monitoring changes in legislation and adjusting policies accordingly

Employee Engagement and Retention:

HR focuses on fostering employee engagement and retention by creating a positive work environment and addressing the needs and concerns of employees. This may involve conducting employee surveys, implementing wellness programs, and promoting worklife balance initiatives. Factors to consider include:
- Building a strong organizational culture
- Encouraging employee involvement and participation
- Recognizing and valuing employee contributions

- Providing opportunities for career development and advancement

Legal Compliance:

HR ensures compliance with labor laws, regulations, and workplace standards to mitigate legal risks and liabilities. This includes staying up to date on employment legislation, maintaining accurate records, and adhering to fair employment practices. Factors to consider include:
- Understanding local, state, and federal labor laws
- Developing and enforcing policies and procedures
- Conducting audits and assessments to ensure compliance
- Seeking legal counsel when necessary

By considering these factors and implementing effective HR practices, businesses can attract, develop, and retain top talent, foster a positive work culture, and achieve their organizational objectives.

Chapter 5.3

Information Technology

Information technology (IT) refers to the use of computers, software, networks, and other digital technologies to store, retrieve, process, and transmit data and information. In a business context, IT plays a crucial role in supporting various business functions, enabling communication, collaboration, automation, and innovation. Here's an overview of information technology and the key factors to consider for business:

Infrastructure and Systems:

IT infrastructure includes hardware, software, networks, and data storage systems that support business operations and processes. Factors to consider include:

Hardware: Computers, servers, networking equipment, and peripherals needed to run business applications and systems.

Software: Operating systems, business applications, productivity tools, and specialized software solutions required to support different functions and workflows.

Networks: Local area networks (LANs), wide area networks (WANs), internet connectivity, and telecommunications infrastructure for data communication and collaboration.

Data Storage: Storage devices, databases, and cloud storage solutions for storing and managing business data and information.

Cybersecurity and Data Protection:

Cybersecurity measures protect business data, systems, and networks from unauthorized access, data breaches, and cyber threats. Factors to consider include:

Access Controls: Implementing user authentication, authorization, and access control mechanisms to restrict access to sensitive data and systems.

Data Encryption: Encrypting data in transit and at rest to prevent unauthorized interception or access.

Firewalls and Intrusion Detection Systems (IDS): Deploying network security appliances and software to monitor and block suspicious network traffic and activities.

Security Policies: Developing and enforcing security policies, procedures, and guidelines to promote security awareness and compliance.

Incident Response: Establishing incident response plans and procedures to detect, respond to, and recover from security incidents or breaches.

Business Applications and Software:

Business applications and software solutions automate and streamline various business processes, improving efficiency, productivity, and decision-making. Factors to consider include:

Enterprise Resource Planning (ERP) Systems: Integrated software platforms that manage core business functions such as finance, accounting, human resources, and supply chain management.

Customer Relationship Management (CRM) Systems: Software solutions for managing customer interactions, sales, marketing, and service delivery.

Productivity Tools: Collaboration tools, project management software, document management systems, and communication platforms that facilitate teamwork and information sharing.

Industry-specific Software: Specialized software applications tailored to specific industries or business needs, such as healthcare, manufacturing, retail, or finance.

Digital Transformation and Innovation:

Digital transformation initiatives leverage IT to drive innovation, optimize processes, and create new business models and revenue streams. Factors to consider include:

Cloud Computing: Adopting cloudbased services and platforms for scalability, flexibility, and cost effectiveness in deploying and managing IT resources.

Internet of Things (IoT): Connecting devices, sensors, and machines to collect data, monitor performance, and automate processes in various industries.

Artificial Intelligence (AI) and Machine Learning: Applying AI and machine learning algorithms to analyze data, make predictions, and automate decision-making in business operations.

Big Data Analytics: Using advanced analytics and data mining techniques to extract insights, identify patterns, and drive datadriven decision-making.

Digital Innovation Labs: Establishing innovation labs or centers of excellence to experiment with emerging technologies and develop new digital solutions and services.

IT Governance and Compliance:

IT governance frameworks and compliance standards ensure that IT investments and activities align with business objectives and regulatory requirements. Factors to consider include:

IT Governance Frameworks: Implementing frameworks such as COBIT, ITIL, or ISO/IEC 2700 to define IT governance structures, processes, and controls.

Regulatory Compliance: Ensuring compliance with industry regulations, data protection laws, and privacy regulations such as GDPR, HIPAA, PCI DSS, and SOX.

Risk Management: Identifying, assessing, and managing IT-related risks that may impact business operations, financial performance, or reputation.

Audits and Assessments: Conducting regular audits, assessments, and reviews to evaluate IT controls, policies, and procedures and address any deficiencies or weaknesses.

User Support and Training:

Providing user support and training ensures that employees have the knowledge and skills to effectively use IT systems and applications. Factors to consider include:

Help Desk and Support Services: Offering help desk support, technical assistance, and troubleshooting services to address user queries and issues.

Training Programs: Developing training materials, courses, and workshops to educate employees on IT systems, applications, and best practices.

User Awareness: Promoting awareness of IT security risks, data protection policies, and safe computing practices to prevent security incidents and data breaches.

Change Management: Managing organizational change and resistance to technology adoption through effective communication, stakeholder engagement, and change management strategies.

Scalability and Flexibility:

IT systems and infrastructure should be scalable and flexible to accommodate changing business needs, growth, and technological advancements. Factors to consider include:

Scalable Architecture: Designing IT systems and solutions with scalability in mind to handle increased workloads, users, and data volumes.

Flexible Deployment Models: Choosing deployment options such as on premises, cloud, or hybrid solutions based on business requirements, cost considerations, and agility.

Modular Design: Adopting modular and interoperable technologies that allow for easy integration, customization, and expansion as business needs evolve.

Vendor and Technology Agnosticism: Avoiding vendor lock in and technology dependencies by selecting open standards, interoperable solutions, and vendor neutral platforms.

Cost Management and ROI:

Managing IT costs effectively and maximizing return on investment (ROI) requires careful planning, budgeting, and monitoring of IT expenditures. Factors to consider include:

Total Cost of Ownership (TCO): Evaluating the full cost of IT investments, including acquisition costs, implementation costs, operating expenses, and maintenance costs.

Cost Benefit Analysis: Assessing the expected benefits and returns of IT projects and initiatives relative to their costs and risks.

Value Realization: Monitoring and measuring the actual business value and outcomes achieved through IT investments, such as increased revenue, cost savings, productivity gains, and customer satisfaction.

Financial Planning and Budgeting: Developing IT budgets, forecasts, and financial plans aligned with business objectives, priorities, and resource constraints.

By considering these factors and effectively leveraging information technology, businesses can improve operational efficiency, enhance customer experiences, drive innovation, and gain a competitive edge in the digital economy.

Chapter 5.4

Customer Service

Customer service is the provision of assistance and support to customers before, during, and after they purchase products or services from a business. It encompasses various interactions and touchpoints between customers and the organization, with the goal of ensuring customer satisfaction, resolving issues, and building long term relationships. Here's an overview of customer service and the key factors to consider for business:

Customer Interaction Channels:

Consider the various channels through which customers may interact with your business, including in person interactions, phone calls, emails, live chat, social media, self service portals, and mobile apps. Ensure that customer service is available through multiple channels to accommodate diverse preferences and needs.

Response Time and Availability:

Provide timely responses to customer inquiries, requests, and complaints. Aim to be readily available and accessible to customers during business hours, and consider offering extended support hours or 24/7 support for critical issues or urgent situations.

Empathy and Communication Skills:

Train customer service representatives to demonstrate empathy, active listening, and effective communication skills when interacting with customers. Encourage them to understand customers' perspectives, acknowledge their concerns, and communicate solutions clearly and courteously.

Product Knowledge and Expertise:

Ensure that customer service representatives possess adequate knowledge and expertise about the products or services offered by the business. Provide comprehensive training and resources to enable them to address customer inquiries, troubleshoot issues, and provide accurate information and guidance.

Problem Resolution and Escalation Procedures:

Establish clear procedures for resolving customer problems and escalating issues as needed. Empower frontline staff to resolve common issues independently, while providing guidelines for escalating complex or unresolved issues to higher level support or management.

Feedback and Continuous Improvement:

Solicit feedback from customers about their experiences with customer service interactions. Monitor customer satisfaction metrics, such as Net Promoter Score (NPS) or customer satisfaction surveys, and use this feedback to identify areas for improvement and implement corrective actions.

Personalization and Customization:

Personalize customer service interactions based on individual preferences, history, and context. Use customer data and insights to tailor responses, recommendations, and offers to meet the unique needs and preferences of each customer.

Consistency and Reliability:

Strive to deliver consistent and reliable customer service experiences across all touchpoints and channels. Ensure that customers receive the same level of service quality and attention regardless of the channel or representative they interact with.

Empowerment and Autonomy:

Empower frontline staff to make decisions and take actions that prioritize customer satisfaction and problem resolution. Provide them with the autonomy and authority to address customer issues promptly and effectively without excessive bureaucracy or approval processes.

Customer Relationship Management (CRM) Systems:

Implement CRM systems or customer service platforms to manage customer interactions, track communication history, and centralize customer information. Use these systems to streamline processes, enhance productivity, and provide personalized service.

Employee Engagement and Recognition:

Foster a culture of employee engagement and recognition within the customer service team. Recognize and reward employees for delivering exceptional customer service, and provide opportunities for professional development and career advancement.

Alignment with Company Values and Brand Promise:

Ensure that customer service practices and behaviors align with the company's values, mission, and brand promise. Demonstrate a commitment to customer centric values and principles throughout the organization, from frontline staff to senior leadership.

By considering these factors and prioritizing customer service excellence, businesses can enhance customer satisfaction, loyalty, and advocacy, ultimately driving longterm success and competitive advantage in the marketplace.

Chapter 6

Policies and Procedures

Policies and procedures are a set of guidelines, rules, and protocols established by a business to govern its operations, activities, and interactions. They provide a framework for decision-making, behavior, and compliance within the organization, ensuring consistency, efficiency, and accountability.

Here's an overview of policies and procedures for business:

Policies:

Policies are formal statements that outline the principles, objectives, and rules that guide decision-making and behavior within the organization. They define expectations, standards, and boundaries for employees and stakeholders. Examples of policies include:

Code of Conduct/Ethics: Defines expected behavior, values, and ethical standards for employees.

Employee Handbook: Provides information about employment terms, benefits, policies, and procedures.

Equal Employment Opportunity (EEO) Policy: Ensures fair treatment and prohibits discrimination and harassment based on protected characteristics.

Data Security and Privacy Policy: Establishes guidelines for protecting sensitive information and ensuring compliance with data protection regulations.

Health and Safety Policy: Defines procedures and responsibilities for maintaining a safe and healthy work environment.

Information Technology (IT) Usage Policy: Sets guidelines for acceptable use of company IT resources, including computers, networks, and software.

Travel and Expense Policy: Establishes guidelines for employee travel, accommodation, and expense reimbursement.

Chapter 6.1

Procedures

Procedures are detailed instructions or steps that outline how specific tasks or activities should be performed to achieve desired outcomes. They provide a standardized approach and ensure consistency and efficiency in operations. Examples of procedures include:

Employee Onboarding Procedure:
Outlines the steps for welcoming and integrating new employees into the organization.

Sales Order Processing Procedure:
Describes the steps for processing sales orders, from receipt to fulfillment and invoicing.

Inventory Management Procedure:
Defines the processes for receiving, storing, tracking, and managing inventory.

Customer Complaint Handling Procedure:
Provides guidelines for addressing and resolving customer complaints in a timely and effective manner.

Performance Appraisal Procedure:
Outlines the process for evaluating employee performance, setting goals, and providing feedback.

Emergency Response Procedure:
Specifies the actions to be taken in the event of emergencies such as fires, natural disasters, or security threats.

IT Security Incident Response Procedure:
Defines the steps for detecting, reporting, and responding to security incidents or breaches.

Procurement Procedure:
Describes the process for sourcing, evaluating, and purchasing goods and services from suppliers.

Key Considerations:

Alignment with Business Objectives:
Policies and procedures should be aligned with the organization's mission, values, and strategic objectives.

Clarity and Accessibility:
Ensure that policies and procedures are clearly written, easily understandable, and readily accessible to employees.

Consistency and Fairness:
Apply policies and procedures consistently and fairly across the organization to promote fairness and avoid favoritism or bias.

Compliance and Legal Requirements:
Ensure that policies and procedures comply with relevant laws, regulations, and industry standards.

Regular Review and Update:
Periodically review and update policies and procedures to reflect changes in laws, regulations, best practices, and organizational needs.

Communication and Training:
Communicate policies and procedures effectively to employees and provide training and guidance to ensure understanding and compliance.

Flexibility and Adaptability:
Allow for flexibility and adaptability in policies and procedures to accommodate changing business needs, market conditions, and technological advancements.

By implementing effective policies and procedures, businesses can establish a framework for governance, compliance, and performance management, promoting consistency, efficiency, and accountability throughout the organization.

Chapter 6.2

Legal and Compliance Policies/ Compliance

Legal and Compliance Policies Legal and compliance policies are essential guidelines and regulations that businesses must adhere to in order to operate lawfully and ethically. These policies ensure that the organization and its employees conduct business in accordance with relevant laws, regulations, industry standards, and ethical principles. Here's an overview of legal and compliance policies, along with key factors to consider for businesses:

Code of Conduct/Ethics:

A code of conduct or ethics outlines the organization's values, principles, and standards of behavior expected from employees. It sets the tone for ethical conduct, integrity, and accountability within the organization.

AntiDiscrimination and Harassment Policies:

These policies prohibit discrimination, harassment, and retaliation based on protected characteristics such as race, gender, age, disability, religion, or sexual orientation. They ensure fair treatment and equal opportunities for all employees.

Data Privacy and Security Policies:

Data privacy and security policies establish guidelines for the collection, use, storage, and protection of sensitive information, including customer data and employee records. They ensure compliance with data protection laws and safeguard against data breaches and unauthorized access.

Intellectual Property Policies:

Intellectual property policies protect the organization's intellectual assets, such as patents, trademarks, copyrights, and trade secrets. They outline procedures for securing intellectual property rights, respecting third-party intellectual property, and preventing infringement.

Employment Laws and Regulations:

Legal and compliance policies should address various employment laws and regulations governing areas such as wages, hours, overtime, leave, benefits, workers' compensation, and employee rights. These policies ensure compliance with labor laws and fair employment practices.

Health and Safety Policies:

Health and safety policies establish procedures for maintaining a safe and healthy work environment, preventing accidents and injuries, and complying with occupational health and safety regulations. They promote employee wellbeing and minimize workplace hazards.

Environmental Compliance Policies:

Environmental compliance policies address environmental laws and regulations related to pollution prevention, waste management, resource conservation, and sustainability practices. They ensure that the organization operates in an environmentally responsible manner.

Financial Reporting and Accounting Policies:

Financial reporting and accounting policies govern financial practices, procedures, and disclosures to ensure accuracy, transparency, and compliance with accounting standards and regulations. They facilitate accurate financial reporting and mitigate financial risks.

Anti-Bribery and Corruption Policies:

Anti-bribery and corruption policies prohibit bribery, corruption, and unethical business practices, and establish controls to prevent bribery and corruption in business operations, transactions, and relationships.

Compliance Training and Awareness:

Provide training and awareness programs to educate employees about legal and compliance policies, their responsibilities, and the consequences of noncompliance. Ensure that employees understand their obligations and know how to report violations or concerns.

Monitoring and Auditing:

Implement monitoring, auditing, and reporting mechanisms to assess compliance with legal and compliance policies, identify potential risks or violations, and take corrective actions as needed.

Legal Counsel and Expertise:

Seek legal counsel and expertise to ensure that legal and compliance policies are up to date, accurate, and aligned with current laws, regulations, and industry standards. Stay informed about changes in legal requirements and emerging compliance issues.

By considering these factors and implementing effective legal and compliance policies, businesses can mitigate legal risks, uphold ethical standards, and maintain trust and credibility with stakeholders.

Chapter 6.3
Financial Policies

Financial policies are a set of guidelines and principles established by a business to govern its financial management practices, decisions, and procedures. These policies help ensure financial stability, efficiency, and transparency, while also promoting accountability and compliance with regulatory requirements. Here's an overview of financial policies and the key factors to consider in business:

Budgeting and Planning:
Financial policies should address the budgeting and planning process, including guidelines for developing annual operating budgets, capital expenditure budgets, and long term financial plans. Factors to consider include:
- Setting budgeting objectives and targets
- Allocating resources effectively
- Monitoring budget performance and variances
- Adjusting budgets as needed based on changing circumstances

Cash Management:
Cash management policies govern the handling, monitoring, and control of cash flows within the organization. They establish procedures for managing cash inflows and outflows, optimizing cash balances, and minimizing liquidity risks. Factors to consider include:
- Maintaining adequate cash reserves
- Managing working capital efficiently
- Implementing cash flow forecasting
- Investing surplus cash prudently

Credit and Receivables Management:
Credit and receivables management policies address the extension

of credit to customers, monitoring of accounts receivable, and collection of outstanding debts. They ensure timely payment from customers and minimize bad debt losses. Factors to consider include:
- Establishing credit terms and conditions
- Evaluating customer creditworthiness
- Implementing credit control measures
- Managing overdue accounts and collections

Financial Reporting and Disclosure:

Financial reporting and disclosure policies govern the preparation, presentation, and dissemination of financial information to internal and external stakeholders. They ensure accuracy, transparency, and compliance with accounting standards and regulations. Factors to consider include:
- Establishing accounting policies and principles
- Producing timely and accurate financial statements
- Disclosing relevant financial information
- Ensuring adherence to regulatory requirements

Investment and Capital Allocation:

Investment and capital allocation policies define criteria and guidelines for making investment decisions, allocating capital to projects, and evaluating investment opportunities. They ensure that capital is deployed effectively to generate returns and create value for shareholders. Factors to consider include:
- Setting investment criteria and risk parameters
- Evaluating investment alternatives
- Prioritizing projects based on strategic objectives
- Monitoring investment performance and outcomes

Risk Management:

Risk management policies address the identification, assessment, mitigation, and monitoring of financial risks that may impact the organization's objectives and operations. They ensure that risks are managed prudently and in accordance with risk tolerance levels. Factors to consider include:
- Identifying financial risks (e.g., market risk, credit risk, liquidity risk)
- Implementing risk management strategies and controls
- Monitoring and reporting on risk exposures
- Establishing contingency plans for risk events

Compliance and Governance:

Financial policies should emphasize compliance with laws, regulations, and internal controls related to financial management and reporting. They promote adherence to ethical standards, accountability, and integrity in financial practices. Factors to consider include:
- Establishing a system of internal controls
- Conducting internal audits and reviews
- Ensuring compliance with regulatory requirements
- Upholding ethical standards and corporate governance principles

Training and Communication:

Provide training and communication programs to ensure that employees understand financial policies, procedures, and responsibilities. Foster a culture of financial literacy and accountability throughout the organization.

Continuous Improvement:

Regularly review and update financial policies to reflect changes in business conditions, regulatory requirements, and best practices. Seek feedback from stakeholders and implement improvements to enhance effectiveness and relevance.

By considering these factors and implementing effective financial policies, businesses can improve financial performance, mitigate risks, and enhance stakeholder confidence and trust.

Chapter 6.4

HR Policies

Human resources (HR) policies are a set of guidelines, principles, and procedures established by a business to govern its management of employees and the workplace environment. These policies ensure compliance with employment laws and regulations, promote fair treatment and consistency, and outline expectations for employee behavior and conduct. Here's an overview of HR policies and the key factors to consider for businesses:

Recruitment and Selection:

Recruitment and selection policies establish guidelines and pro-

cedures for attracting, evaluating, and hiring qualified candidates. Factors to consider include:
- Job posting and advertising strategies
- Candidate sourcing and screening methods
- Interviewing and selection criteria
- Background checks and reference checks

Employee Classification and Compensation:

Employee classification and compensation policies define job classifications, salary structures, pay scales, and benefits packages. Factors to consider include:
- Job descriptions and classifications
- Compensation benchmarking and salary surveys
- Payroll administration and deductions
- Employee benefits (e.g., health insurance, retirement plans, paid time off)

Employee Onboarding and Orientation:

Onboarding and orientation policies outline the process for welcoming and integrating new employees into the organization. Factors to consider include:
- Orientation programs and activities
- Provision of company information and resources
- Training and development opportunities
- Mentorship and buddy systems

Performance Management and Appraisal:

Performance management and appraisal policies establish procedures for setting performance expectations, conducting evaluations, and providing feedback to employees. Factors to consider include:
- Performance goals and objectives
- Performance evaluation criteria and rating scales
- Performance appraisal forms and processes
- Performance improvement plans (PIPs) and development goals

Training and Development:

Training and development policies address employee learning and skill development opportunities. Factors to consider include:
- Training needs assessment
- Training programs and initiatives
- Training delivery methods (e.g., workshops, online courses)
- Professional development and career advancement pathways

Employee Relations and Conduct:

Employee relations and conduct policies govern workplace behavior, interactions, and disciplinary procedures. Factors to consider include:
- Code of conduct and ethics
- Antidiscrimination and harassment policies
- Grievance and dispute resolution procedures
- Disciplinary actions and progressive discipline

Leave and Attendance:

Leave and attendance policies address employee absences, leaves of absence, and time off. Factors to consider include:
- Types of leave (e.g., vacation, sick leave, parental leave)
- Leave eligibility and accruals
- Leave request and approval processes
- Attendance tracking and reporting

Health and Safety:

Health and safety policies ensure a safe and healthy work environment for employees. Factors to consider include:
- Workplace health and safety regulations
- Hazard identification and risk assessment
- Accident/incident reporting and investigation
- Emergency preparedness and response

Confidentiality and Data Protection:

Confidentiality and data protection policies safeguard sensitive information and ensure compliance with privacy laws and regulations. Factors to consider include:
- Confidentiality agreements and nondisclosure agreements (NDAs)
- Data privacy and security measures
- Handling of employee and customer data
- Data breach response and notification procedures

Remote Work and Flexible Work Arrangements:

Remote work and flexible work arrangements policies address the guidelines and procedures for remote work, telecommuting, and flexible scheduling options. Factors to consider include:
- Eligibility criteria and approval processes
- Remote work equipment and technology requirements
- Communication and collaboration guidelines

- Performance expectations and accountability

Compliance and Legal Considerations:

Ensure that HR policies comply with applicable employment laws, regulations, and industry standards. Stay updated on changes in legislation and seek legal counsel as needed to ensure compliance.

Communication and Training:

Communicate HR policies effectively to employees and provide training and guidance on policy interpretation and implementation. Foster a culture of compliance, fairness, and transparency.

Review and Evaluation:

Regularly review and evaluate HR policies to ensure relevance, effectiveness, and alignment with organizational goals and objectives. Seek feedback from employees and stakeholders and make adjustments as needed.

By considering these factors and implementing effective HR policies, businesses can promote a positive work environment, foster employee engagement and satisfaction, and ensure legal compliance and organizational effectiveness.

Chapter 6.5

IT Policies Information Technology

IT Policies Information technology (IT) policies are guidelines and procedures established by a business to govern the use, management, and security of information technology resources and assets. These policies ensure the effective and secure use of technology systems, networks, and data, while also promoting compliance with regulatory requirements and industry standards. Here's an overview of IT policies and the key factors to consider:

Acceptable Use Policy (AUP):

An acceptable use policy defines acceptable and prohibited uses of IT resources, including computers, networks, internet access, and software applications. Factors to consider include:
- Guidelines for appropriate use of technology resources

- Prohibited activities (e.g., unauthorized access, malware distribution)
- Consequences of policy violations
- User responsibilities and accountability

Information Security Policy:

An information security policy outlines measures to protect the confidentiality, integrity, and availability of information assets. Factors to consider include:
- Data classification and handling guidelines
- Access controls and authentication requirements
- Encryption and data protection measures
- Incident response and reporting procedures

Password Management Policy:

A password management policy establishes rules for creating, managing, and securing user passwords and credentials. Factors to consider include:
- Password complexity requirements
- Password expiration and rotation policies
- Multifactor authentication (MFA) requirements
- Secure storage and transmission of passwords

Data Backup and Recovery Policy:

A data backup and recovery policy defines procedures for regularly backing up critical data and systems, as well as restoring data in the event of data loss or system failure. Factors to consider include:
- Backup frequency and schedules
- Data retention periods
- Offsite storage and disaster recovery strategies
- Testing and verification of backups

Network Security Policy:

A network security policy outlines measures to protect network infrastructure and data transmission. Factors to consider include:
- Network segmentation and access controls
- Firewall and intrusion detection/prevention systems (IDS/IPS)
- Virtual private network (VPN) usage guidelines
- Wireless network security protocols (e.g., WPA2, WPA3)

Software and Application Usage Policy:

A software and application usage policy governs the installation,

usage, and licensing of software applications on company devices. Factors to consider include:
- Authorized software and applications
- Prohibited software installations (e.g., unauthorized downloads)
- Software license compliance
- Patch management and software updates

Mobile Device Management (MDM) Policy:

An MDM policy addresses the use of mobile devices (e.g., smartphones, tablets) in the workplace and establishes security measures to protect corporate data on these devices. Factors to consider include:
- Device registration and enrollment procedures
- Mobile device security settings (e.g., device encryption, remote wipe)
- Bring Your Own Device (BYOD) policies
- Mobile application management (MAM) guidelines

Remote Access Policy:

A remote access policy defines guidelines and requirements for accessing company networks and resources remotely. Factors to consider include:
- Remote access authentication methods (e.g., VPN, SSH)
- Access control measures (e.g., user roles and permissions)
- Security awareness training for remote workers
- Monitoring and auditing of remote access activities

Social Media and Internet Usage Policy:

A social media and internet usage policy governs the use of social media platforms and internet resources by employees. Factors to consider include:
- Guidelines for social media use in the workplace
- Restrictions on accessing inappropriate or non work related websites
- Protection of company reputation and confidentiality
- Employee privacy considerations

Compliance and Regulatory Requirements:

Ensure that IT policies comply with relevant laws, regulations, and industry standards, such as data protection regulations (e.g., GDPR, CCPA), industry specific compliance requirements (e.g., HIPAA for healthcare), and cybersecurity frameworks (e.g., NIST Cybersecurity Framework).

Training and Awareness:
Provide training and awareness programs to educate employees about IT policies, cybersecurity best practices, and their roles and responsibilities in protecting company assets and data.

Regular Review and Updates:
Regularly review and update IT policies to reflect changes in technology, business processes, regulatory requirements, and emerging cybersecurity threats. Ensure that policies remain relevant and effective in addressing current challenges and risks.

By considering these factors and implementing effective IT policies, businesses can enhance cybersecurity, protect sensitive data, and ensure the reliable and secure use of technology resources to support business operations.

Chapter 6.6
Customer Service Policies

Customer service policies are a set of guidelines and principles established by a business to govern its interactions with customers and ensure the delivery of high quality service. These policies define the standards, expectations, and procedures for addressing customer needs, resolving issues, and fostering positive relationships. Here's an overview of customer service policies and the key factors to consider for businesses:

Customer Engagement and Interaction:
Customer engagement policies outline how employees should interact with customers across various channels, including in person interactions, phone calls, emails, live chat, social media, and self service portals. Factors to consider include:
- Greeting and welcoming customers
- Active listening and empathy
- Professionalism and courtesy
- Timely responses and follow-ups

Service Quality and Standards:
Service quality policies establish standards and expectations for

delivering high-quality service to customers. Factors to consider include:
- Service excellence goals and objectives
- Service level agreements (SLAs)
- Performance metrics and targets
- Continuous improvement initiatives

Issue Resolution and Escalation:

Issue resolution and escalation policies define procedures for handling customer complaints, inquiries, and issues in a timely and effective manner. Factors to consider include:
- Acknowledging and validating customer concerns
- Resolving issues promptly and satisfactorily
- Escalating unresolved issues to higherlevel support or management
- Offering compensation or remedies when appropriate

Product Knowledge and Expertise:

Product knowledge and expertise policies ensure that employees possess adequate knowledge about the products or services offered by the business to assist customers effectively. Factors to consider include:
- Training programs and resources
- Product information and specifications
- Frequently asked questions (FAQs) and troubleshooting guides
- Access to subject matter experts for complex inquiries

Communication and Transparency:

Communication and transparency policies promote clear and transparent communication with customers regarding products, services, pricing, policies, and procedures. Factors to consider include:
- Providing accurate and consistent information
- Communicating service updates and changes
- Being transparent about pricing, fees, and terms
- Managing customer expectations effectively

Privacy and Confidentiality:

Privacy and confidentiality policies ensure the protection of customer information and data privacy rights. Factors to consider include:
- Safeguarding sensitive customer data
- Obtaining consent for data collection and use

- Complying with data protection laws and regulations
- Handling customer information securely and responsibly

Accessibility and Inclusivity:

Accessibility and inclusivity policies ensure that services are accessible and inclusive for customers with disabilities or diverse needs. Factors to consider include:
- Providing accommodations for customers with disabilities
- Offering multilingual support
- Ensuring website and digital accessibility
- Training employees on diversity and inclusion

Feedback and Continuous Improvement:

Feedback and continuous improvement policies solicit feedback from customers about their experiences with customer service interactions and use it to drive improvements. Factors to consider include:
- Customer satisfaction surveys and feedback mechanisms
- Analyzing feedback and identifying areas for improvement
- Implementing changes based on customer feedback
- Monitoring customer satisfaction metrics and trends

Employee Empowerment and Autonomy:

Employee empowerment and autonomy policies empower frontline staff to make decisions and take actions that prioritize customer satisfaction and problem resolution. Factors to consider include:
- Providing authority and discretion to employees
- Encouraging initiative and creativity in customer interactions
- Supporting employees with resources and tools
- Recognizing and rewarding exceptional customer service

Compliance and Legal Considerations:

Ensure that customer service policies comply with relevant laws, regulations, and industry standards, such as consumer protection laws and regulations governing customer data privacy.

Training and Development:

Provide training and development programs to equip employees with the skills, knowledge, and competencies needed to deliver exceptional customer service and adhere to customer service policies.

Regular Review and Updates:

Regularly review and update customer service policies to reflect changes in customer needs, market dynamics, and emerging trends, ensuring that policies remain relevant and effective in meeting customer expectations.

By considering these factors and implementing effective customer service policies, businesses can enhance customer satisfaction, loyalty, and retention, ultimately driving long term success and competitive advantage in the marketplace.

Chapter 6.7

Key Performance Indicators (KPIs)

Key Performance Indicators (KPIs) are quantifiable metrics used to measure the performance and effectiveness of various aspects of a business in achieving its objectives and goals. KPIs provide valuable insights into the health, progress, and success of the business, allowing stakeholders to monitor performance, identify areas for improvement, and make data driven decisions. Here's an overview of key performance indicators for business across different functional areas:

Financial KPIs:

Revenue Growth Rate: Measures the percentage increase in revenue over a specific period.

Profit Margin: Calculates the percentage of revenue that translates into profit after accounting for expenses.

Return on Investment (ROI): Evaluates the profitability of an investment by comparing the return generated to the cost of the investment.

Cash Flow: Tracks the movement of cash in and out of the business to ensure sufficient liquidity.

Operating Expenses Ratio: Compares total operating expenses to revenue to assess efficiency in cost management.

Sales and Marketing KPIs:

Sales Revenue: Measures the total revenue generated from sales of products or services.

Customer Acquisition Cost (CAC): Calculates the cost incurred to acquire a new customer.

Customer Lifetime Value (CLV): Estimates the total revenue a customer is expected to generate over their entire relationship with the business.

Conversion Rate: Tracks the percentage of leads or prospects that convert into paying customers.

Marketing Return on Investment (ROI): Assesses the effectiveness of marketing campaigns by comparing the revenue generated to the cost of marketing activities.

Customer Service KPIs:

Customer Satisfaction Score (CSAT): Measures the level of satisfaction among customers based on their experience with the business.

Net Promoter Score (NPS): Determines the likelihood of customers to recommend the business to others.

First Response Time: Tracks the average time taken to respond to customer inquiries or complaints.

Resolution Time: Measures the average time taken to resolve customer issues or requests.

Customer Retention Rate: Calculates the percentage of customers retained over a specific period.

Operations and Production KPIs:

Productivity: Measures the output or efficiency of production processes, often expressed as units produced per hour or labor cost per unit.

Inventory Turnover Ratio: Calculates the number of times inventory is sold and replaced within a given period.

OnTime Delivery Performance: Tracks the percentage of orders or shipments delivered on time to customers.

Quality Yield: Measures the percentage of defect free products or services produced.

Equipment Downtime: Tracks the amount of time equipment is out of operation due to maintenance or breakdowns.

Human Resources KPIs:

Employee Turnover Rate: Calculates the percentage of employees who leave the organization over a specific period.

Employee Engagement Score: Measures the level of employee engagement and satisfaction within the organization.

Training Hours per Employee: Tracks the average number of training hours provided to employees.

Absenteeism Rate: Measures the percentage of scheduled work hours missed by employees due to absence.

TimetoFill: Tracks the average time taken to fill vacant positions within the organization.

Information Technology (IT) KPIs:

Uptime Percentage: Measures the availability and reliability of IT systems and infrastructure.

Mean Time to Repair (MTTR): Tracks the average time taken to repair or resolve IT incidents or outages.

System Performance: Monitors the performance and responsiveness of IT systems and applications.

Security Incident Rate: Measures the frequency of security incidents or breaches affecting IT assets.

IT Project Success Rate: Calculates the percentage of IT projects completed successfully within budget and schedule.

Strategic KPIs:

Market Share: Measures the percentage of total market sales or revenue captured by the business.

Brand Awareness: Tracks the level of recognition and awareness of the business brand among target audiences.

Customer Acquisition Rate: Measures the rate at which new customers are acquired by the business.

Innovation Index: Assesses the level of innovation and creativity within the organization.

Chapter 6.7

Strategic Objective Achievement: Tracks progress towards achieving strategic goals and objectives outlined in the business's strategic plan.

Now as we have identified KPI's, lets dig deeper understand that when selecting KPIs for a business, it's essential to consider factors such as relevance to business objectives, measurability, reliability of data sources, and alignment with stakeholders' interests. Additionally, KPIs should be tracked consistently over time to monitor trends and identify areas for improvement. Lets look into the mechanics of KPi's

Chapter 6.8
Measurement and Reporting Process

The measurement and reporting process in business involves the systematic collection, analysis, and presentation of data and key performance indicators (KPIs) to assess organizational performance, monitor progress toward goals, and inform decision-making. This process enables businesses to track their performance, identify areas for improvement, and make data driven decisions to drive success.

Here's an overview of the measurement and reporting process and factors to consider:

Define Objectives and KPIs:
Clearly define organizational objectives, goals, and targets that align with the business strategy. Identify relevant KPIs that measure progress toward these objectives and establish targets or benchmarks for each KPI.

Data Collection and Aggregation:
Gather relevant data from various sources, including internal systems, databases, surveys, and external sources. Ensure the accuracy, completeness, and timeliness of data by implementing data quality controls and validation processes.

Data Analysis and Interpretation:
Analyze the collected data to derive meaningful insights and trends. Use statistical analysis, data visualization techniques, and comparative analysis to interpret the data and identify patterns, correlations, and outliers.

Performance Monitoring and Tracking:

Monitor and track KPIs on an ongoing basis to assess performance against targets or benchmarks. Use dashboards, scorecards, and reporting tools to visualize KPIs and provide real time insights into performance.

Identify Trends and Patterns:

Identify trends, patterns, and anomalies in the data that may indicate areas of strength or areas for improvement. Look for correlations between different KPIs and factors that may impact performance.

Root Cause Analysis:

Conduct root cause analysis to understand the underlying factors contributing to performance outcomes. Identify the drivers or factors influencing KPI performance and determine corrective actions to address issues.

Benchmarking and Comparison:

Benchmark performance against industry standards, best practices, or competitors to assess relative performance and identify opportunities for improvement. Compare performance across different business units, teams, or time periods to identify outliers and areas for focus.

Report Generation and Distribution:

Generate comprehensive reports and presentations that communicate performance insights, trends, and recommendations to key stakeholders. Customize reports to meet the needs of different audiences and distribute them through appropriate channels.

Frequency and Timing:

Determine the frequency and timing of reporting based on the relevance and urgency of the information. Regularly scheduled reports may be appropriate for tracking ongoing performance, while adhoc reports may be needed for specific analyses or decision-making.

Data Security and Confidentiality:

Ensure the security and confidentiality of data throughout the measurement and reporting process. Implement data governance policies, access controls, and encryption methods to protect sensitive information from unauthorized access or disclosure.

Continuous Improvement:

Continuously evaluate and improve the measurement and reporting process to enhance efficiency, accuracy, and relevance. Solicit feedback from stakeholders, automate repetitive tasks, and leverage technology solutions to streamline the process.

Training and Skills Development:

Provide training and development opportunities to employees involved in the measurement and reporting process to enhance their data analysis, visualization, and communication skills. Foster a culture of data literacy and accountability within the organization.

By considering these factors and implementing an effective measurement and reporting process, businesses can gain valuable insights into their performance, drive continuous improvement, and achieve their strategic objectives.

Chapter 6.9
Targets and Benchmarks

Targets and benchmarks are quantitative goals or reference points that businesses set to measure progress, guide decision-making, and assess performance against desired outcomes. These targets provide a clear direction for the organization and help ensure alignment with strategic objectives. Factors to consider when setting targets and benchmarks for business include:

Strategic Objectives:

Targets and benchmarks should be directly aligned with the organization's strategic objectives and goals. Consider how achieving specific targets contributes to broader business priorities and mission.

Measurability:

Ensure that targets and benchmarks are measurable and quantifiable. Use key performance indicators (KPIs) and relevant metrics to track progress and assess performance objectively.

Specificity:

Clearly define targets and benchmarks with specific, concrete criteria. Avoid ambiguity and ensure that targets are well defined, achievable, and actionable.

Realism and Attainability:

Set targets and benchmarks that are realistic and attainable within the given time frame and resource constraints. Consider factors such as market conditions, competitive landscape, and available resources.

Time Frame:

Define a clear time frame for achieving targets and benchmarks. Determine whether targets are short term, medium term, or long term, and establish deadlines or milestones for progress monitoring.

Baseline Data:

Use historical data or baseline performance metrics as a reference point when setting targets and benchmarks. Analyze past performance trends and identify areas for improvement to inform target setting.

External Factors:

Consider external factors and market dynamics that may impact the achievement of targets, such as economic conditions, industry trends, regulatory changes, and competitive pressures.

Internal Capabilities:

Assess the organization's internal capabilities, strengths, and weaknesses when setting targets and benchmarks. Consider factors such as operational efficiency, technological infrastructure, and workforce skills.

Stakeholder Input:

Seek input and feedback from key stakeholders, including employees, customers, investors, and partners, when setting targets and benchmarks. Ensure alignment with stakeholders' expectations and priorities.

Continuous Monitoring and Adjustment:

Continuously monitor progress toward targets and benchmarks and be prepared to adjust them as needed based on changing circumstances, emerging opportunities, or unforeseen challenges.

Stretch Goals:

Consider setting stretch goals or aspirational targets that challenge the organization to achieve higher levels of performance and innovation. Stretch goals can inspire motivation and drive breakthrough results.

Communication and Accountability:

Communicate targets and benchmarks clearly and transparently to all stakeholders, and establish accountability mechanisms to ensure ownership and responsibility for achieving targets across the organization.

By considering these factors and setting targets and benchmarks effectively, businesses can create a roadmap for success, drive performance improvement, and achieve sustainable growth and success.

Chapter 7

Technology and Tools Technology

Technology and Tools Technology and tools play a crucial role in modern business operations, enabling organizations to streamline processes, enhance productivity, improve decision-making, and gain a competitive edge. Here are some essential technology categories and tools commonly used in businesses:

Communication and Collaboration Tools

Email Services: Platforms like Microsoft Outlook, Gmail, or corporate email servers facilitate internal and external communication.

Instant Messaging Apps: Tools like Slack, Microsoft Teams, or Skype enable real time messaging, file sharing, and collaboration among teams.

Video Conferencing Software: Platforms like Zoom, Microsoft Teams, or Google Meet allow remote teams to conduct virtual meetings, webinars, and presentations.

Project Management Software: Tools like Trello, Asana, or Jira help teams plan, organize, and track project tasks, deadlines, and progress.

Productivity Software

Office Suites: Software suites like Microsoft Office (Word, Excel, PowerPoint) or Google Workspace offer tools for document creation, spreadsheets, presentations, and collaboration.

NoteTaking Apps: Platforms like Evernote, OneNote, or Notion allow users to capture, organize, and share notes, ideas, and tasks across devices.

Task Management Apps: Tools like Todoist, Wunderlist, or Microsoft To Do help individuals and teams manage tasks, priorities, and deadlines effectively.

Customer Relationship Management (CRM) Systems

CRM platforms like Salesforce, HubSpot, or Zoho CRM enable businesses to manage customer interactions, sales leads, marketing campaigns, and customer data effectively.

Enterprise Resource Planning (ERP) Systems:

ERP software solutions like SAP, Oracle, or Microsoft Dynamics integrate core business processes such as finance, inventory management, supply chain, human resources, and manufacturing into a unified system.

Data Analytics and Business Intelligence (BI) Tools:

BI platforms like Tableau, Power BI, or Google Data Studio allow businesses to analyze, visualize, and gain insights from large volumes of data to support decision-making and strategic planning.

Cloud Computing Services:

Cloud platforms like Amazon Web Services (AWS), Microsoft Azure, or Google Cloud Platform offer scalable computing resources, storage, and infrastructure as a service (IaaS), enabling businesses to deploy and manage applications and data in the cloud.

Cybersecurity Solutions:

Antivirus and Malware Protection: Software solutions like McAfee, Norton, or Bitdefender help protect devices and networks from viruses, malware, and cyber threats.

Firewall and Network Security: Hardware and software firewalls, VPNs, and intrusion detection/prevention systems (IDS/IPS) safeguard networks and data from unauthorized access and cyber attacks.

Identity and Access Management (IAM): IAM solutions manage user identities, permissions, and access controls to ensure secure authentication and authorization.

Ecommerce Platforms:

Ecommerce platforms like Shopify, WooCommerce, or Magento enable businesses to create and manage online stores, process transactions, and sell products or services to customers worldwide.

Customer Support and Helpdesk Software:

Helpdesk and ticketing systems like Zendesk, Freshdesk, or ServiceNow streamline customer support operations, ticket management, and issue resolution through various channels (e.g., email, chat, phone).

Business Process Automation (BPA) Tools:

BPA platforms like Zapier, Integromat, or Microsoft Power Automate automate repetitive tasks, workflows, and processes across different applications and systems to improve efficiency and reduce manual effort.

These are just some examples of technology and tools used in businesses across various industries. The choice of technology depends on the specific needs, requirements, and goals of each organization. Additionally, businesses should consider factors such as scalability, integration capabilities, security, usability, and cost effectiveness when selecting and implementing technology solutions.

Chapter 7.1
Software and Systems Used

Software and Systems Used Software and systems are essential components of modern businesses, enabling organizations to streamline operations, enhance productivity, and achieve strategic objectives. Here are some common types of software and systems used in business operations, along with factors to consider when selecting and implementing them:

Enterprise Resource Planning (ERP) Systems:

ERP systems integrate core business processes such as finance, human resources, supply chain management, and customer relationship management into a centralized database and unified platform. Factors to consider are:
- Scalability to accommodate future growth and expansion.
- Flexibility to customize modules and workflows to meet specific business needs.
- Integration capabilities with existing systems and thirdparty applications.
- User friendliness and ease of training for employees.

Customer Relationship Management (CRM) Systems:

CRM systems manage customer interactions, sales leads, marketing campaigns, and customer data to improve customer satisfaction and drive sales growth. Factors to consider:
- Ability to track and analyze customer interactions across multiple channels.
- Customization options to tailor workflows and processes to match business requirements.
- Mobile accessibility for sales teams to access customer data on the go.
- Data security and compliance with privacy regulations (e.g., GDPR, CCPA).

Accounting and Financial Management Software:

Accounting software automates financial processes such as bookkeeping, invoicing, payroll, and financial reporting to ensure accurate and timely financial management. Factors to consider:
- Compliance with accounting standards and regulations (e.g., GAAP, IFRS).
- Integration with banks, payment gateways, and tax filing systems.
- Advanced features for budgeting, forecasting, and financial analysis.
- Data encryption and secure storage of sensitive financial information.

Human Resources Management Systems (HRMS):

HRMS software automates HR processes such as employee onboarding, payroll processing, performance management, and workforce planning to optimize HR efficiency and employee engagement. Factors to consider:
- Comprehensive HR functionalities covering recruitment, talent management, and employee development.
- Integration with time and attendance systems for accurate payroll processing.
- Compliance with labor laws and regulations regarding employee data privacy and security.
- Self service portals for employees to access HR information and services.

Collaboration and Communication Tools:

Collaboration tools facilitate communication, file sharing, and

project collaboration among team members, regardless of location. Factors to consider:
- Realtime messaging, video conferencing, and screen sharing capabilities.
- Integration with email, calendar, and productivity apps for seamless workflow.
- Security features such as end to end encryption and access controls.
- Mobile accessibility for remote work and on the go collaboration.

Document Management Systems (DMS):

DMS software organizes, stores, and manages electronic documents and files, improving document security, version control, and accessibility. Factors to consider:
- Scalability to accommodate growing volumes of documents and data.
- Search and retrieval capabilities to quickly locate and access documents.
- Version control and audit trails to track document changes and revisions.
- Integration with workflow automation tools for streamlined document approval processes.

Business Intelligence (BI) and Analytics Platforms:

BI and analytics platforms enable organizations to analyze and visualize data to gain insights, make informed decisions, and drive business performance. Factors to consider:
- Data integration capabilities to consolidate data from multiple sources.
- Advanced analytics features such as predictive modeling and machine learning.
- Interactive dashboards and reports for data visualization and exploration.
- Scalability to handle large datasets and complex analytical queries.

Project Management Software:

Project management software helps plan, organize, and track project tasks, timelines, and resources to ensure project success and collaboration among team members. Factors to consider:
- Task management features such as task assignment, scheduling,and progress tracking.

- Resource allocation and workload balancing to optimize team productivity.
- Collaboration tools for document sharing, discussion forums, and project communication.
- Integration with other tools and systems used in project workflows.

When selecting and implementing software and systems for business operations, it's important to consider factors such as functionality, usability, scalability, integration capabilities, security, compliance, cost effectiveness, and alignment with organizational goals and processes. Additionally, involving key stakeholders and conducting thorough evaluations, pilots, and training programs can help ensure successful adoption and utilization of the chosen software and systems within the organization.

Chapter 7.2

Training and Support Resources

Training and support resources are critical components for ensuring the successful implementation, adoption, and utilization of new software, systems, or processes within a business. Effective training and support help employees develop the necessary skills and knowledge to use tools effectively, troubleshoot issues, and maximize productivity. Here are some key factors to consider when planning training and support resources for business:

Training Needs Assessment:

Conduct a thorough assessment to identify the training needs of employees based on their roles, skill levels, and familiarity with the new software or system. Determine the specific knowledge gaps and training objectives to address through training programs.

Training Methods and Formats:

Choose appropriate training methods and formats that suit the learning preferences and needs of employees. Options may include:
- Instructor led training (inperson or virtual)
- Handson workshops or interactive sessions
- Online self paced courses or tutorials

- Video demonstrations or screencasts
- Job aids, cheat sheets, or user manuals

Customization and Tailoring:

Customize training content and materials to align with the specific features, functionalities, and use cases relevant to employees' roles and responsibilities. Tailor training programs to address the unique challenges and requirements of different departments or teams within the organization.

Engagement and Participation:

Foster engagement and active participation in training sessions by making them interactive, relevant, and engaging. Incorporate practical examples, case studies, and handson exercises to reinforce learning and encourage participation.

Training Schedule and Timing:

Plan training sessions at times that minimize disruption to regular work activities and accommodate employees' availability and schedules. Consider offering flexible training options such as staggered sessions or recorded sessions for employees in different time zones or with varying shifts.

Ongoing Support and Resources:

Provide ongoing support and resources to help employees apply their learning and address questions or challenges that arise during the transition period. Offer access to helpdesk support, online forums, knowledge bases, and user communities where employees can seek assistance and share best practices.

Feedback and Evaluation:

Gather feedback from employees regarding the effectiveness of training programs, content, and delivery methods. Use surveys, focus groups, or feedback forms to solicit input and identify areas for improvement. Continuously evaluate training outcomes and make adjustments as needed to enhance effectiveness.

Train the Trainer Programs:

Empower internal subject matter experts or "super users" to serve as trainers or mentors who can provide ongoing support and assistance to their colleagues. Implement train the trainer programs to equip these individuals with the necessary knowledge and skills to deliver effective training sessions.

Integration with Performance Management:

Integrate training and skill development initiatives with performance management processes to link training outcomes with employee performance and development goals. Encourage employees to apply their newly acquired skills and knowledge in their daily work activities and recognize their achievements.

Continuous Learning Culture:

Foster a culture of continuous learning and skill development within the organization by promoting opportunities for professional growth and advancement. Encourage employees to pursue further training, certifications, or skill building activities to stay updated and relevant in their roles.

Budget and Resources Allocation:

Allocate sufficient budget and resources for training and support initiatives, including expenses related to training materials, instructor fees, technology infrastructure, and ongoing support services. Ensure that training investments align with business priorities and strategic objectives.

By considering these factors and implementing comprehensive training and support resources, businesses can empower employees to adapt to changes, embrace new technologies, and contribute to organizational success effectively.

Chapter 7.3

Data Security Measures

Data security measures are critical for businesses to protect sensitive information from unauthorized access, disclosure, alteration, or destruction. Implementing robust data security measures helps safeguard confidential data, maintain customer trust, and comply with regulatory requirements. Here are key data security measures and factors to consider for businesses:

Access Control:

Limit access to sensitive data based on the principle of least privilege, ensuring that only authorized individuals have access to the data they need to perform their job roles.

Implement strong authentication methods such as passwords, multifactor authentication (MFA), biometrics, or smart cards to verify the identity of users accessing the data.

Regularly review and update user access rights and permissions to align with changes in job roles, responsibilities, and employee status (e.g., new hires, terminations).

Data Encryption:

Encrypt sensitive data at rest (stored data) and in transit (data being transmitted over networks) using strong encryption algorithms and protocols.

Implement end to end encryption for communications and data exchanges between systems, applications, and devices to protect against eavesdropping and interception.

Use encryption key management practices to securely generate, store, distribute, and rotate encryption keys to prevent unauthorized access to encrypted data.

Network Security:

Deploy firewalls, intrusion detection/prevention systems (IDS/IPS), and network segmentation techniques to protect the network perimeter and detect/respond to unauthorized access attempts or malicious activities.

Secure wireless networks with strong encryption (e.g., WPA2/WPA3), network access controls, and regular monitoring for rogue access points or unauthorized devices.

Implement virtual private networks (VPNs) to encrypt data transmitted over public networks and provide secure remote access to corporate resources for employees working remotely.

Endpoint Security:

Install and maintain antivirus/antimalware software on endpoints (e.g., computers, laptops, mobile devices) to detect and remove malicious software threats such as viruses, ransomware, and spyware.

Implement endpoint detection and response (EDR) solutions to continuously monitor and analyze endpoint activity for signs of suspicious behavior or security incidents.

Enforce device encryption, strong password policies, and remote wipe capabilities for lost or stolen devices to protect sensitive data stored on endpoints.

Data Loss Prevention (DLP):

Deploy DLP solutions to monitor, classify, and prevent the unauthorized transfer, sharing, or leakage of sensitive data across endpoints, networks, and cloud services.

Implement data masking or redaction techniques to anonymize or obfuscate sensitive information in documents, databases, or reports shared internally or externally.

Educate employees about data handling best practices and security policies to prevent accidental data breaches or violations.

Security Training and Awareness:

Provide regular security training and awareness programs to educate employees about common cyber threats, phishing attacks, social engineering tactics, and security best practices.

Conduct simulated phishing exercises to test employees' awareness and response to phishing attempts and provide targeted training based on the results.

Foster a culture of security awareness and accountability where employees understand their roles and responsibilities in protecting data and reporting security incidents promptly.

Incident Response and Management:

Develop and implement an incident response plan that outlines procedures for detecting, assessing, containing, and responding to security incidents such as data breaches, malware infections, or unauthorized access.

Establish a dedicated incident response team or designate individuals responsible for coordinating incident response efforts, conducting investigations, and communicating with stakeholders.

Conduct regular tabletop exercises or simulated incident scenarios to test the effectiveness of the incident response plan and ensure readiness to respond to real world incidents.

Regulatory Compliance:

Understand and comply with relevant data protection regulations, industry standards, and compliance requirements applicable to your business (e.g., GDPR, HIPAA, PCI DSS).

Conduct regular compliance assessments and audits to evaluate adherence to regulatory requirements, identify gaps or vulnerabilities, and implement corrective actions to address noncompliance issues.

Maintain documentation of data security policies, procedures, risk assessments, and compliance efforts to demonstrate accountability and due diligence to regulators, customers, and stakeholders.

Vendor Risk Management:

Evaluate the security practices and capabilities of third party vendors, suppliers, and service providers that have access to or handle sensitive data on behalf of the business.

Establish contractual agreements and service level agreements (SLAs) with vendors that define security requirements, responsibilities, and expectations regarding data protection and privacy.

Monitor and assess vendor compliance with security requirements through regular audits, security assessments, and performance reviews.

Data Backup and Recovery:

Implement regular data backup procedures to create copies of critical data and systems and store them securely in offsite or cloud based backup repositories.

Test backup and recovery processes periodically to ensure data integrity, availability, and recoverability in the event of data loss, corruption, or ransomware attacks.

Develop a comprehensive data recovery plan that outlines procedures for restoring operations, recovering data, and minimizing downtime in the event of a disaster or cybersecurity incident.

By implementing these data security measures and considering the associated factors, businesses can strengthen their defenses against cyber threats, protect sensitive information, and mitigate the risks of data breaches or security incidents. Additionally, fostering a culture of security awareness and continuous improvement can further enhance the organization's resilience to evolving cybersecurity threats and challenges.

Chapter 8

Training and Development

Training and development for businesses refer to processes and activities designed to enhance the skills, knowledge, abilities, and competencies of employees to improve their performance, productivity, and effectiveness in their roles. Training and development initiatives aim to align employees' skills with organizational goals, foster a culture of continuous learning, and support career growth and advancement. Here are key aspects of training and development for businesses:

Training Needs Assessment:

Conduct a thorough assessment to identify the current skills, knowledge gaps, and training needs of employees based on their job roles, responsibilities, and performance objectives.

Use performance evaluations, skills assessments, employee feedback, and organizational goals to determine the specific training requirements and priorities.

Training Strategy and Planning:

Develop a comprehensive training strategy and plan that outlines the goals, objectives, target audience, training methods, resources, and timelines for delivering training programs.

Align training initiatives with organizational priorities, business objectives, and workforce development strategies to ensure relevance and effectiveness.

Training Delivery Methods:

Choose appropriate training delivery methods and formats based on the learning preferences, needs, and constraints of employees. Common training delivery methods include:
- Instructor led training (classroom or virtual)
- Online or elearning courses
- Interactive workshops or seminars
- On the job training or apprenticeships
- Peer learning or mentoring programs

Content Development and Curriculum Design:

Develop and design training content and curriculum that cover relevant topics, skills, and competencies needed to perform job roles effectively.

Incorporate interactive learning activities, case studies, simulations, and real world examples to engage learners and reinforce learning objectives.

Ensure that training materials are up to date, accurate, and accessible to employees through learning management systems (LMS) or training portals.

Skill Development Programs:

Offer skill development programs and workshops focused on specific areas such as leadership development, communication skills, technical skills, customer service, project management, and industry specific competencies.

Provide opportunities for employees to acquire new skills, certifications, or credentials relevant to their job roles and career aspirations.

Career Development and Advancement:

Support employees' career development and advancement through training and development initiatives that enhance their capabilities, expand their professional network, and prepare them for future roles and responsibilities.

Offer career planning resources, coaching, and mentoring programs to help employees set career goals, identify development opportunities, and navigate their career paths within the organization.

Continuous Learning Culture:

Foster a culture of continuous learning and skill development within the organization by promoting opportunities for ongoing education, training, and professional growth.

Encourage employees to take ownership of their learning and development by providing access to self directed learning resources, online courses, and developmental assignments.

Evaluation and Measurement:

Evaluate the effectiveness and impact of training and development programs through feedback mechanisms, assessments, and performance evaluations.

Measure key performance indicators (KPIs) such as employee

engagement, job satisfaction, productivity, and skills proficiency to assess the return on investment (ROI) of training initiatives.

Use evaluation findings to identify areas for improvement, refine training strategies, and adjust learning interventions to better meet the needs of employees and the organization.

Leadership Development:

Invest in leadership development programs to cultivate leadership competencies and capabilities at all levels of the organization.

Provide leadership training, coaching, and mentoring to develop future leaders, empower managers to lead effectively, and foster a culture of leadership excellence.

Employee Engagement and Recognition:

Recognize and reward employees who actively participate in training and development initiatives, demonstrate commitment to continuous learning, and apply newly acquired skills in their roles.

Celebrate achievements, milestones, and successes in training and development to reinforce a culture of learning, growth, and excellence.

By investing in training and development for employees, businesses can enhance employee satisfaction, retention, and performance, build a skilled and capable workforce, and gain a competitive advantage in the marketplace. Additionally, fostering a culture of continuous learning and development can contribute to organizational agility, innovation, and long term success.

Chapter 8.1

Onboarding Process

The onboarding process refers to the systematic process of integrating new employees into the organization and preparing them for their roles, responsibilities, and the company culture. A well-designed onboarding process can contribute to higher employee engagement, satisfaction, and retention, as well as faster productivity and performance. Here are the key components and factors to consider for an effective onboarding process in business:

Preboarding Preparation:

Communicate with the new employee before their start date to provide essential information about the onboarding process, required documentation, and any preemployment tasks or paperwork to complete.

Set up their workspace, equipment, access to systems and tools, and any necessary resources or materials they'll need on their first day.

Welcome and Introduction:

Greet the new employee warmly on their first day and provide a tour of the workplace, introducing them to colleagues, team members, and key stakeholders.

Provide an overview of the company's mission, values, culture, and organizational structure to help the new employee understand the company's vision and how their role contributes to it.

Orientation and Training:

Conduct an orientation session to familiarize the new employee with company policies, procedures, benefits, and HR related matters such as payroll, benefits enrollment, and workplace policies.

Provide job specific training and on-the-job learning opportunities to help the new employee develop the skills, knowledge, and competencies required to perform their role effectively.

Clarification of Expectations:

Set clear expectations for the new employee regarding their roles, responsibilities, performance objectives, and key performance indicators (KPIs). Discuss performance goals, milestones, and evaluation criteria to align expectations and foster accountability.

Buddy or Mentor Program:

Assign a buddy, mentor, or peer mentor to the new employee to provide guidance, support, and assistance during their onboarding period. The buddy can help answer questions, facilitate introductions, and offer insights into company culture and norms.

Feedback and Check Ins:

Schedule regular check in meetings with the new employee to provide feedback, address any concerns or questions, and assess their progress and adjustment to the role and organization.

Encourage open communication and solicit feedback from the new employee about their onboarding experience, areas for improvement, and suggestions for enhancing the process.

Integration and Socialization:

Facilitate opportunities for the new employee to socialize and build relationships with colleagues through teambuilding activities, departmental meetings, social events, and networking opportunities.

Encourage participation in employee resource groups, affinity groups, or professional development initiatives to help the new employee feel connected and engaged with the organization.

Continuous Support and Development:

Provide ongoing support, coaching, and resources to help the new employee navigate challenges, overcome obstacles, and succeed in their role.

Offer opportunities for career development, skill enhancement, and professional growth through training programs, mentorship, and career advancement pathways.

Evaluation and Feedback:

Conduct a formal evaluation of the onboarding process to assess its effectiveness, identify areas for improvement, and gather feedback from key stakeholders, including the new employee, managers, HR, and colleagues.

Use evaluation findings to refine and enhance the onboarding process, address gaps or issues, and ensure continuous improvement over time.

Factors to consider when designing and implementing an onboarding process for business include:

Customization: Tailor the onboarding process to meet the unique needs, preferences, and backgrounds of new employees, considering factors such as role, experience level, cultural differences, and learning styles.

Consistency: Ensure consistency and standardization in the onboarding process across departments, locations, and roles to provide a cohesive and unified experience for new employees.

Technology Integration: Leverage technology solutions such as onboarding software, learning management systems (LMS), and digital platforms to automate and streamline onboarding tasks, workflows, and communications.

Flexibility and Adaptability: Design a flexible onboarding process that can accommodate different start dates, remote work arrangements, and changing business needs or circumstances.

Feedback Loop: Establish mechanisms for gathering feedback from new employees, managers, and stakeholders to assess the effectiveness of the onboarding process and identify areas for improvement.

Compliance and Legal Requirements: Ensure compliance with relevant labor laws, regulations, and industry standards governing onboarding practices, data privacy, and employment documentation.

Timeframe and Duration: Define a clear timeline and duration for the onboarding process, balancing the need for thorough orientation and training with the desire to expedite the new employee's integration and productivity.

Manager Involvement: Engage managers and supervisors in the onboarding process to provide guidance, support, and feedback to new employees and reinforce their role in facilitating a positive onboarding experience.

By considering these components and factors, businesses can create an onboarding process that effectively integrates new employees, accelerates their time to productivity, and fosters long term engagement and retention.

Chapter 8.2

Ongoing Training Programs

Ongoing training programs, also known as continuous learning or professional development initiatives, are essential for businesses to help employees stay updated on industry trends, acquire new skills, enhance job performance, and adapt to changing job roles and responsibilities. These programs contribute to employee satisfaction, engagement, and retention, as well as organizational growth and competitiveness. Here are key components and factors to consider when designing and implementing ongoing training programs for business:

Training Needs Analysis:
Conduct regular assessments to identify emerging skill gaps, training needs, and areas for improvement among employees based

on changes in job requirements, technology advancements, industry trends, and business goals.

Gather feedback from employees, managers, and stakeholders to understand their learning preferences, career aspirations, and training priorities.

Alignment with Business Objectives:

Ensure that ongoing training programs are aligned with the strategic goals, priorities, and evolving needs of the organization. Link training initiatives to key performance indicators (KPIs) and business outcomes to demonstrate the value and impact of training investments.

Tailor training content and objectives to support organizational initiatives such as new product launches, process improvements, technology adoptions, or market expansion.

Diverse Learning Opportunities:

Offer a variety of learning modalities and formats to accommodate different learning styles, preferences, and schedules. Mix traditional classroom training, online courses, webinars, workshops, conferences, and on the job learning experiences.

Provide self paced learning resources, microlearning modules, and just In time training materials that employees can access anytime, anywhere to support continuous learning and skill development.

Subject Matter Experts and External Resources:

Tap into internal subject matter experts (SMEs), industry leaders, and external training providers to deliver specialized training workshops, seminars, or guest lectures on relevant topics and emerging trends.

Encourage cross functional collaboration and knowledge sharing among employees by facilitating peer learning, communities of practice, or lunch and learn sessions.

Technology Integration:

Leverage technology solutions such as learning management systems (LMS), online training platforms, virtual classrooms, and mobile learning apps to deliver, track, and manage ongoing training programs efficiently.

Explore emerging technologies such as augmented reality (AR), virtual reality (VR), and gamification to create immersive and engaging learning experiences that enhance retention and engagement.

Continuous Feedback and Evaluation:

Establish mechanisms for gathering feedback from participants and stakeholders to assess the effectiveness, relevance, and impact of ongoing training programs.

Use evaluation data, participant surveys, course completion rates, and performance metrics to measure learning outcomes, identify areas for improvement, and refine training content and delivery methods.

Manager Support and Involvement:

Engage managers and supervisors in supporting and promoting ongoing training initiatives by communicating the importance of employee development, encouraging participation, and providing resources and time for learning activities.

Equip managers with the skills and tools they need to coach, mentor, and support their team members' ongoing learning and development journey.

Recognition and Rewards:

Recognize and reward employees who actively participate in ongoing training programs, demonstrate a commitment to learning, and apply newly acquired skills in their roles.

Celebrate achievements, milestones, and certifications attained through ongoing training efforts to reinforce a culture of continuous learning and acknowledge employees' dedication to personal and professional growth.

Career Development Pathways:

Integrate ongoing training programs with career development pathways, talent management, and succession planning initiatives to provide employees with opportunities for advancement, skill progression, and career growth.

Offer career counseling, coaching, and development planning support to help employees identify their career goals, acquire the necessary skills, and pursue advancement opportunities within the organization.

Budget and Resource Allocation:

Allocate sufficient budget, resources, and time for ongoing training programs, including expenses related to course materials, instructor fees, technology infrastructure, and employee time away from regular duties.

Prioritize training investments based on strategic priorities, business needs, and potential return on investment (ROI) in terms of improved employee performance, productivity, and retention.

By considering these factors and implementing ongoing training programs effectively, businesses can foster a culture of continuous learning and development, empower employees to succeed in their roles, and maintain a competitive edge in the marketplace. Ongoing training initiatives contribute to organizational agility, innovation, and resilience by equipping employees with the skills and knowledge they need to adapt to changing business environments and drive business success.

Chapter 8.3
Career Development Opportunities

Career development opportunities are initiatives and programs designed to support employees in advancing their careers, acquiring new skills, and achieving their professional goals within the organization. Providing career development opportunities not only fosters employee engagement and retention but also contributes to organizational success by cultivating a skilled and motivated workforce. Here are key components and factors to consider when offering career development opportunities in business:

Career Pathways and Advancement:

Define clear career pathways and advancement opportunities within the organization, outlining potential progression routes, role transitions, and promotion criteria for employees.

Communicate career paths and advancement opportunities to employees through career development discussions, performance reviews, and talent management processes.

Skills Development and Training:

Offer training programs, workshops, and courses that support skill development and competency enhancement in areas relevant to employees' current roles and future career aspirations.

Provide access to professional development resources, certifications, and learning opportunities that align with employees' career goals and the organization's strategic objectives.

Mentorship and Coaching:

Establish formal mentorship programs that pair employees with experienced mentors or coaches who can provide guidance, support, and advice on career development, skill acquisition, and professional growth.

Encourage informal mentoring relationships and peer coaching among employees to facilitate knowledge sharing, skill transfer, and career networking.

Job Rotation and Cross Functional Assignments:

Offer opportunities for employees to gain exposure to different roles, departments, and projects through job rotation programs, temporary assignments, or cross functional teams.

Rotate employees through challenging assignments, stretch projects, or special initiatives that broaden their skills, expand their experience, and prepare them for future leadership roles.

Performance Feedback and Development Planning:

Provide regular performance feedback and coaching to employees to help them identify strengths, areas for improvement, and opportunities for growth.

Collaborate with employees to create individual development plans (IDPs) that outline specific goals, objectives, and action steps for career advancement and skill development.

Leadership Development Programs:

Offer leadership development programs and initiatives to prepare high potential employees for future leadership roles within the organization.

Provide leadership training, executive coaching, and mentoring opportunities to develop key leadership competencies such as communication, decision-making, strategic thinking, and team building.

Recognition and Rewards:

Recognize and reward employees who demonstrate exceptional performance, leadership potential, or contributions to the organization's success through career advancement, promotions, awards, or special recognition programs.

Link career progression and advancement opportunities with performance based rewards, compensation adjustments, and benefits to incentivize employee engagement and commitment.

Succession Planning and Talent Management:

Implement succession planning processes to identify and develop high potential talent within the organization for key leadership positions and critical roles.

Build a talent pipeline by proactively identifying and grooming successors for key positions through targeted development initiatives, career planning, and performance management strategies.

Work Life Balance and Flexibility:

Support employees' career development goals by offering flexible work arrangements, telecommuting options, and work life balance initiatives that accommodate their personal commitments and professional aspirations.

Provide resources and support for employees to manage work related stress, burnout, and wellbeing while pursuing career development opportunities.

Diversity, Equity, and Inclusion (DEI):

Ensure that career development opportunities are accessible and equitable for all employees, regardless of background, identity, or demographic factors.

Promote diversity and inclusion in leadership development programs, succession planning, and talent management initiatives to foster a culture of belonging and equal opportunity for career advancement.

Employee Engagement and Feedback:

Solicit feedback from employees on their career development needs, aspirations, and experiences through surveys, focus groups, and one-on-one discussions.

Actively involve employees in career planning discussions, performance reviews, and development planning to ensure alignment between individual career goals and organizational objectives.

Continuous Improvement and Evaluation:

Continuously evaluate the effectiveness of career development programs and initiatives through metrics such as employee engagement, retention rates, promotion rates, and talent pipeline strength.

Collect feedback from employees, managers, and stakeholders to identify areas for improvement, refine program offerings, and enhance the overall employee experience.

By considering these factors and implementing effective career development opportunities, businesses can empower employees to grow, succeed, and contribute to the organization's longterm success. Career development initiatives not only enhance employee engagement and retention but also strengthen the organization's talent pipeline, leadership bench strength, and competitive advantage in the marketplace.

Chapter 9
Communication and Collaboration

Communication and collaboration are essential components of effective teamwork and organizational success in business. Here's an overview of communication and collaboration in business, along with factors to consider:

Communication:

Communication refers to the exchange of information, ideas, thoughts, and messages between individuals or groups within an organization. It encompasses verbal, nonverbal, written, and digital communication channels.

Importance:

Effective communication fosters clarity, understanding, alignment, and coordination among team members, departments, and stakeholders. It facilitates decision-making, problem solving, conflict resolution, and relationship building within the organization.

Channels:

Communication can occur through various channels, including face to face meetings, emails, phone calls, instant messaging, video conferencing, memos, presentations, and collaboration tools/platforms.

Factors to Consider:

Clarity and Conciseness: Ensure messages are clear, concise, and easily understood by the intended audience to minimize misinterpretation and confusion.

Active Listening: Encourage active listening skills among employees to promote understanding, empathy, and engagement in communication exchanges.

Feedback Mechanisms: Establish feedback loops and mechanisms for soliciting input, ideas, and opinions from employees, fostering a culture of open communication and continuous improvement.

Timeliness and Responsiveness: Emphasize the importance of timely communication and responsiveness to inquiries, requests, and feedback to maintain efficiency and avoid delays.

Cultural and Diversity Considerations: Recognize and respect cultural differences, language barriers, and diversity within the organization, adapting communication strategies to accommodate diverse perspectives and backgrounds.

Collaboration: Collaboration involves individuals or groups working together cooperatively to achieve common goals, solve problems, and accomplish tasks or projects. It requires sharing knowledge, resources, and responsibilities to leverage collective expertise and achieve synergistic outcomes.

Importance: Collaboration promotes innovation, creativity, and synergy by harnessing the diverse skills, perspectives, and talents of team members. It enhances decision-making, problem solving, and adaptability, leading to improved performance and results.

Tools and Technologies: Collaboration tools and technologies facilitate virtual collaboration and teamwork by providing platforms for document sharing, real time communication, project management, and workflow automation. Examples include project management software, document collaboration tools, video conferencing platforms, and enterprise social networks.

Factors to Consider:

Team Dynamics: Foster a collaborative culture that values teamwork, trust, mutual respect, and shared accountability among team members. Encourage open communication, idea sharing, and constructive feedback to build strong team dynamics.

Clear Goals and Roles: Define clear objectives, roles, and responsibilities for team members to ensure alignment and clarity about project expectations and deliverables.

Transparent Processes: Establish transparent processes, workflows, and decision-making frameworks to facilitate collaboration and ensure accountability. Document and communicate procedures, guidelines, and best practices to guide collaborative efforts.

Conflict Resolution: Develop conflict resolution strategies and mechanisms to address disagreements, misunderstandings, or conflicts that may arise during collaboration. Encourage respectful dialogue, active listening, and compromise to resolve conflicts constructively and maintain positive relationships.

Recognition and Rewards: Recognize and reward collaborative efforts, teamwork, and contributions to reinforce desired behaviors and motivate employees to collaborate effectively.

Effective communication and collaboration are integral to building strong relationships, driving innovation, and achieving organizational goals. By fostering a culture of open communication, active collaboration, and shared purpose, businesses can leverage the collective intelligence and talents of their workforce to achieve sustainable success.

Chapter 9.1
Internal Communication Channels

Internal communication channels in business are the pathways or mediums through which information, messages, and updates are exchanged among employees, teams, and departments within an organization. These channels play a crucial role in facilitating collaboration, alignment, transparency, and engagement among employees, contributing to organizational effectiveness and success. Here are common internal communication channels in business and factors to consider for their effective implementation:

Face to Face Communication

In person meetings, team huddles, one on one discussions, and informal conversations are examples of face to face communication channels. These interactions allow for immediate feedback, nonverbal cues, and personal connections.

Factors to Consider:

Frequency and Accessibility: Schedule regular team meetings, departmental gatherings, and town hall sessions to facilitate face to face communication and foster a sense of belonging and community among employees.

Open Door Policy: Encourage an open door policy where employees feel comfortable approaching managers, supervisors, or colleagues for discussions, feedback, or support without barriers or formalities.

Active Listening: Promote active listening skills among employees to ensure effective communication and understanding during face to face interactions. Encourage attentive listening, empathy, and validation of others' perspectives and concerns.

Written Communication

Written communication channels include emails, newsletters, memos, intranet posts, company announcements, and formal documents such as policies, procedures, and reports. These channels convey information in a structured and documented format.

Factors to Consider:

Clarity and Consistency: Ensure written messages are clear, concise, and consistent in tone, style, and formatting to enhance readability and comprehension among recipients.

Audience Segmentation: Tailor written communications to the specific needs, interests, and preferences of different employee groups, departments, or job roles to maximize relevance and impact.

Timeliness and Relevance: Deliver timely and relevant information through written communications to keep employees informed about important updates, initiatives, events, and organizational changes.

Digital Communication Tools

Digital communication tools encompass a wide range of platforms and technologies that enable real time or asynchronous communication, collaboration, and information sharing. Examples include instant messaging apps, collaboration platforms, project management tools, and enterprise social networks.

Factors to Consider:

Tool Selection and Integration: Choose digital communication tools that align with the organization's needs, goals, and infrastructure. Select user friendly platforms that support seamless integration, interoperability, and scalability.

Training and Adoption: Provide training and support to employees to familiarize them with digital communication tools and encourage their adoption and proficiency. Offer resources, tutorials, and best practices to facilitate effective usage.

Security and Privacy: Ensure that digital communication tools comply with data security and privacy regulations and implement safeguards to protect sensitive information from unauthorized access, breaches, or misuse.

Formal Meetings and Presentations

Formal meetings, such as departmental meetings, project reviews, training sessions, and presentations, provide structured forums for sharing information, discussing key topics, and making decisions.

Factors to Consider:

Agenda and Objectives: Set clear agendas, objectives, and expectations for formal meetings to ensure focused discussions and efficient use of participants' time.

Participation and Engagement: Encourage active participation and engagement from attendees by soliciting input, asking questions, and facilitating interactive discussions or brainstorming sessions.

Follow Up and Action Items: Document meeting minutes, action items, and decisions made during formal meetings and communicate them promptly to relevant stakeholders. Establish accountability for followup tasks and deadlines to ensure progress and closure.

Feedback and Suggestion Channels:

Feedback and suggestion channels provide avenues for employees to share their opinions, ideas, concerns, and suggestions with management, HR, or relevant stakeholders. These channels can include suggestion boxes, feedback surveys, suggestion forums, or dedicated email addresses.

Factors to Consider:

Accessibility and Anonymity: Ensure that feedback and suggestion channels are easily accessible to all employees and offer options for anonymous submission to encourage honest and candid feedback.

Responsiveness and Transparency: Acknowledge and respond to feedback and suggestions in a timely manner, demonstrating a commitment to listening, addressing concerns, and implementing actionable recommendations where feasible.

Continuous Improvement: Use feedback and suggestions received through these channels to identify opportunities for process improvement, innovation, and employee engagement initiatives. Communicate updates and outcomes to employees to demonstrate that their input is valued and acted upon.

Social Events and Informal Gatherings:

Social events, teambuilding activities, and informal gatherings provide opportunities for employees to connect, build relationships, and engage in casual conversations outside of work related contexts.

Factors to Consider:

Inclusivity and Diversity: Organize social events and gatherings that are inclusive, diverse, and accessible to all employees, regardless of their backgrounds, interests, or preferences.

Team Bonding and Morale: Use social events and informal gatherings to foster team bonding, boost morale, and create a sense of camaraderie and belonging among employees.

Balance and Flexibility: Offer a variety of social events and activities that cater to different interests, preferences, and schedules. Allow for flexibility in participation to accommodate diverse needs and priorities.

Leadership Communication:

Description: Leadership communication channels involve communication from senior leaders, executives, and managers to disseminate strategic direction, organizational goals, performance updates, and important announcements.

Factors to Consider:

Transparency and Authenticity: Maintain transparency and authenticity in leadership communication by providing honest, candid, and timely updates on key issues, challenges, and successes facing the organization.

Two Way Communication: Encourage two way communication between leaders and employees by soliciting feedback, answering questions, and addressing concerns raised by employees through various channels.

Visibility and Accessibility: Ensure that senior leaders are visible, approachable, and accessible to employees through regular communication forums, such as town hall meetings, Q&A sessions, or informal meet and greets.

Factors to Consider for Effective Internal Communication Channels:

Consistency and Frequency: Establish regular communication rhythms and schedules to ensure consistent and timely delivery of information across all channels.

Accessibility and Inclusivity: Make internal communication channels accessible to all employees, including remote workers, parttime employees, and those with disabilities. Ensure that communication materials are available in multiple formats and languages to accommodate diverse needs.

Measurement and Evaluation: Implement metrics and key performance indicators (KPIs) to track the effectiveness, reach, and engagement of internal communication channels. Use feedback, surveys, and analytics to assess employee satisfaction, comprehension, and responsiveness to communication efforts.

Integration and Alignment: Integrate internal communication channels with broader organizational initiatives, goals, and values to reinforce alignment and consistency in messaging. Coordinate communication efforts across departments and teams to ensure coherence and minimize redundancy or conflicting information.

By considering these factors and implementing a diverse mix of internal communication channels, businesses can foster a culture of transparency, collaboration, and engagement, enhancing employee morale, productivity, and organizational performance. Effective internal communication channels help build trust, strengthen relationships, and empower employees to contribute to the achievement of organizational goals and objectives.

Chapter 9.2

Team Collaboration Tools

Team collaboration tools in business are software platforms and applications designed to facilitate communication, coordination, and cooperation among team members working on projects, tasks, or initiatives. These tools provide centralized platforms for sharing information, collaborating on documents, managing tasks, and communicating in real time, regardless of team members' locations or time zones. Here are some common types of team collaboration tools used in business:

Project Management Platforms:

Description: Project management platforms enable teams to plan, organize, track, and manage projects from initiation to completion. They provide features such as task assignment, milestone tracking, Gantt charts, and progress reporting.

Examples: Asana, Trello, Monday.com, Basecamp, Jira.

Document Collaboration Tools:

Document collaboration tools allow teams to create, edit, review, and share documents collaboratively in real time. They support version control, commenting, and file sharing features to streamline document collaboration.

Examples: Google Workspace (formerly G Suite), Microsoft 365 (formerly Office 365), Dropbox Paper, Quip, Confluence.

Communication and Messaging Apps:

Description: Communication and messaging apps facilitate real time communication and instant messaging among team members. They support text based chat, voice calls, video conferencing, and file sharing features to enhance team collaboration and connectivity.

Examples: Slack, Microsoft Teams, Google Chat, Discord, Zoom.

Virtual Meeting and Video Conferencing Tools:

Virtual meeting and video conferencing tools enable teams to conduct remote meetings, presentations, and video conferences with participants from different locations. They provide features such as screen sharing, recording, and virtual backgrounds.

Examples: Zoom, Microsoft Teams, Google Meet, GoToMeeting, Cisco Webex, .

Collaborative Document Editing Tools:

Collaborative document editing tools allow multiple users to work on the same document simultaneously, making real time edits, comments, and annotations. They support collaborative editing of text documents, spreadsheets, presentations, and diagrams.

Examples: Google Docs, Microsoft Office Online, Zoho Docs, Notion, Overleaf (for LaTeX documents).

File Storage and Sharing Platforms:

File storage and sharing platforms provide centralized repositories for storing, organizing, and sharing files and documents securely. They offer features such as file synchronization, access controls, and version history.

Examples: Google Drive, Dropbox, Microsoft OneDrive, Box, SharePoint.

Task and Workflow Automation Tools:

Task and workflow automation tools streamline repetitive tasks, processes, and workflows by automating routine actions and notifications. They help improve efficiency, consistency, and productivity by reducing manual effort and minimizing errors.

Examples: Zapier, Microsoft Power Automate, IFTTT (If This, Then That), Automate.io, Workato.

Collaborative Whiteboarding Tools:

Collaborative whiteboarding tools enable teams to brainstorm ideas, visualize concepts, and collaborate on diagrams, charts, and sketches in real time. They provide digital whiteboard canvases and drawing tools for collaborative ideation and problem solving.

Examples: Miro, MURAL, Microsoft Whiteboard, Lucidchart, Sketchboard.

Knowledge Management Platforms:

Knowledge management platforms centralize and organize organizational knowledge, information, and resources for easy access and retrieval. They facilitate knowledge sharing, documentation, and collaboration among team members.

Examples: Confluence, Notion, Tettra, Slab, Bit.ai.

Collaborative Code Editing and Version Control Tools:

Collaborative code editing and version control tools enable software developers to collaborate on coding projects, manage source code repositories, and track changes to codebase collaboratively.

Examples: GitHub, GitLab, Bitbucket, Visual Studio Code Live Share, CodePen.

When selecting team collaboration tools for business, consider factors such as ease of use, integration capabilities, security features, scalability, cost, and compatibility with existing workflows and technologies. Implementing the right mix of collaboration tools can enhance teamwork, communication, productivity, and innovation within your organization.

Chapter 9.3
Meetings and Reporting Structure

Meetings and reporting structures are essential components of organizational communication and decision-making processes in business. They provide frameworks for sharing information, discussing key topics, aligning goals, and monitoring progress towards objectives. Here's an overview of meetings and reporting structures in business, along with factors to consider for their effective implementation:

Meetings

Meetings serve various purposes, including brainstorming, problem solving, decision-making, status updates, project planning, and team collaboration. They provide opportunities for face to face or virtual interactions among team members, stakeholders, and leaders.

Types of Meetings

Common types of meetings in business include:

Regular Team Meetings: Scheduled meetings for teams to discuss progress, challenges, and priorities.

Project Meetings: Meetings focused on specific projects or initiatives to review status, milestones, and action items.

One on One Meetings: Individual meetings between managers and team members to provide feedback, coaching, and support.

Departmental Meetings: Meetings involving members of a department or functional area to coordinate activities and address department specific issues.

Cross Functional Meetings: Meetings involving representatives from different departments or teams to collaborate on cross functional projects or initiatives.

Factors to Consider:

Agenda: Define a clear agenda with specific topics, objectives, and time allocations to guide the meeting discussion and ensure focus.

Attendance: Invite relevant stakeholders and decision-makers to participate in the meeting while avoiding unnecessary attendees to optimize productivity.

Facilitation: Assign a meeting facilitator or moderator responsible for guiding the discussion, managing time, and ensuring participation from all attendees.

Engagement: Encourage active participation, collaboration, and engagement from attendees by soliciting input, asking questions, and fostering open dialogue.

Action Items: Document action items, decisions, and next steps during the meeting and assign responsibilities to individuals with clear deadlines and follow up mechanisms.

Follow Up: Send meeting minutes, summaries, or action item lists to attendees promptly after the meeting to reinforce accountability and keep stakeholders informed.

Reporting Structures

Reporting structures define hierarchical relationships, roles, and responsibilities within the organization. They establish lines of authority, communication, and accountability for decision-making and performance management.

Types of Reporting Structures

Hierarchical Structure: Traditional pyramid shaped structure with clear levels of authority and reporting relationships from top management to frontline employees.

Matrix Structure: Hybrid structure where employees report to both functional managers (e.g., department heads) and project managers or team leaders.

Flat Structure: Structure with fewer hierarchical layers and more decentralized decision-making and autonomy among employees.

Functional Structure: Structure organized by functions or departments (e.g., marketing, finance, operations) with reporting lines within each functional area.

Factors to Consider:

Clarity: Ensure clarity and transparency in reporting relationships, roles, and expectations to avoid confusion and ambiguity among employees.

Alignment: Align reporting structures with organizational goals, strategies, and objectives to facilitate coordination and integration across departments and teams.

Communication Channels: Establish clear communication channels and protocols for reporting information, updates, and performance metrics up and down the reporting hierarchy.

Flexibility: Adapt reporting structures to accommodate organizational changes, growth, or shifts in priorities while maintaining clarity and accountability.

Empowerment: Empower employees with decision-making authority, autonomy, and accountability within their roles to foster ownership and initiative.

Feedback Mechanisms: Implement feedback mechanisms and performance evaluation processes to provide regular feedback, coaching, and support to employees within the reporting structure.

By considering these factors and implementing effective meetings and reporting structures, businesses can enhance communication, collaboration, and alignment across the organization, driving productivity, innovation, and success. Meetings and reporting structures serve as essential tools for fostering transparency, accountability, and continuous improvement within the business environment.

Chapter 10

Crisis Management and Contingency Plans

Risk assessment for business involves identifying, analyzing, and evaluating potential risks that could affect the achievement of business objectives. It's a systematic process that helps businesses understand their risk exposure and make informed decisions about how to manage and mitigate those risks. Here's an overview of the key components of risk assessment for business:

Identifying Risks:

Identify potential risks that could impact the organization's ability to achieve its objectives. These risks can come from various sources, including internal processes, external events, strategic decisions, compliance issues, and changes in the business environment.

Consider a wide range of risk categories, such as operational, financial, strategic, compliance, legal, reputational, and cybersecurity risks.

Analyzing Risks:

Assess the likelihood and potential impact of each identified risk on the organization's objectives. This involves analyzing the probability of occurrence and the severity of the consequences if the risk were to materialize.

Consider the interdependencies between different risks and how they could compound or mitigate each other's effects.

Evaluating Risks:

Evaluate the significance of each identified risk based on its likelihood and potential impact. This involves prioritizing risks according to their importance and determining which risks require immediate attention and action.

Consider the organization's risk appetite and tolerance levels, as well as its capacity to absorb and manage risk.

Risk Mitigation and Management:

Develop strategies and measures to mitigate and manage identified risks. This may involve implementing controls, safeguards, and preventive measures to reduce the likelihood or impact of risks.

Consider various risk management techniques, such as risk avoidance, risk reduction, risk transfer, and risk acceptance.

Assign responsibility for managing and monitoring specific risks to appropriate individuals or teams within the organization.

Monitoring and Review:

Continuously monitor and review the effectiveness of risk management strategies and controls.

Regularly reassess and update the risk assessment to reflect changes in the business environment, internal processes, and emerging risks.

Maintain open communication channels to ensure that stakeholders are aware of risks and actively engaged in risk management efforts.

By conducting risk assessments, businesses can proactively identify and address potential threats to their success, enhance decision-making processes, and improve their overall resilience to uncertainty and adversity. Risk assessment is an ongoing process that should be integrated into the organization's strategic planning and management practices.

Chapter 10.1

Emergency Response Procedures

Emergency response procedures for business outline the steps and actions that employees and stakeholders should take in the event of an emergency or crisis situation. These procedures are designed to ensure the safety of individuals, protect property and assets, and minimize the impact of the emergency on business operations. Here's an overview of the key components of emergency response procedures for business:

Emergency Preparedness Planning:

Develop an emergency response plan that identifies potential emergency scenarios (e.g., fire, natural disasters, active shooter) and outlines specific procedures for each scenario.

Establish an emergency response team responsible for implementing and coordinating the plan.

Conduct regular training and drills to ensure that employees are familiar with emergency procedures and know how to respond effectively.

Emergency Communication:

Establish communication protocols and channels for notifying employees, customers, suppliers, and other stakeholders in the event of an emergency.

Designate individuals or teams responsible for initiating and managing communication during an emergency.

Ensure that communication methods are reliable and accessible, including backup systems in case primary methods fail.

Evacuation Procedures:

Develop evacuation procedures for safely evacuating employees and visitors from the premises in the event of a fire, gas leak, or other immediate threat.

Identify evacuation routes and assembly areas where individuals should gather after evacuating.

Assign responsibilities to designated individuals (e.g., floor wardens, evacuation coordinators) to assist with evacuations and account for all personnel.

Shelter in Place Procedures:

Establish shelter in place procedures for situations where it is safer for individuals to remain indoors, such as during severe weather or a hazardous materials incident.

Identify designated shelter areas within the facility and provide instructions for securing the area and minimizing exposure to external threats.

Emergency Response Teams and Roles:

Designate specific roles and responsibilities for members of the emergency response team, including incident commanders, safety coordinators, first aid responders, and communications liaisons.

Ensure that team members receive appropriate training and resources to fulfill their roles effectively.

Emergency Services Coordination:

Establish protocols for contacting and coordinating with emergency services (e.g., fire department, police, medical responders) during an emergency.

Provide emergency responders with access to relevant information about the facility and any hazardous materials present.

Post Emergency Recovery:

Develop procedures for assessing damage, conducting safety inspections, and resuming normal operations after an emergency.

Assign responsibility for documenting and reporting any injuries, property damage, or environmental impacts resulting from the emergency.

Review and debrief after each emergency to identify lessons learned and areas for improvement in the response procedures.

By implementing comprehensive emergency response procedures, businesses can enhance their ability to protect lives and property, maintain business continuity, and recover quickly from emergencies or disasters. It's essential to regularly review and update these procedures to reflect changes in the business environment, organizational structure, and emergency response best practices.

Chapter 10.2

Business Continuity Planning

Business Continuity Planning (BCP) is the process of developing strategies and procedures to ensure that essential business functions can continue during and after a disaster or disruptive event. The goal of BCP is to minimize the impact of disruptions on business operations and to facilitate the organization's ability to recover quickly and efficiently. Here's an overview of the key components and steps involved in business continuity planning:

Risk Assessment and Business Impact Analysis (BIA):

Identify potential risks and threats that could disrupt business operations, such as natural disasters, cyber attacks, power outages, or pandemics.

Conduct a business impact analysis to assess the potential consequences of these disruptions, including financial losses, operational downtime, and damage to reputation.

Developing a Business Continuity Plan:

Define the objectives and scope of the business continuity plan.

Establish a BCP team or committee responsible for developing and implementing the plan.

Identify critical business functions, processes, and resources that must be protected and prioritized for recovery.

Develop strategies and procedures for maintaining or restoring these critical functions during and after a disruption.

Emergency Response and Incident Management:

Develop an emergency response plan outlining procedures for responding to immediate threats and ensuring the safety of employees and stakeholders.

Establish incident management protocols for assessing the severity of disruptions, activating the BCP, and coordinating response efforts.

Backup and Recovery:

Implement backup systems and procedures for critical data, applications, and infrastructure.

Establish offsite backup locations or cloud based solutions to ensure redundancy and data resilience.

Develop recovery strategies and timelines for restoring operations to normal levels following a disruption.

Communication and Notification:

Establish communication channels and protocols for notifying employees, customers, suppliers, and other stakeholders during a crisis.

Develop procedures for disseminating timely and accurate information to keep stakeholders informed of the situation and recovery efforts.

Training and Awareness:

Provide training and awareness programs to ensure that employees understand their roles and responsibilities in implementing the BCP.

Conduct regular drills and exercises to test the effectiveness of the plan and identify areas for improvement.

Continuous Improvement and Review:

Regularly review and update the business continuity plan to reflect changes in the business environment, technology, and risks.

Conduct post incident reviews and lessons learned sessions to identify strengths and weaknesses in the response and recovery process.

By implementing a robust business continuity plan, organizations can enhance their resilience to disruptions and improve their ability to adapt and recover in the face of unforeseen events.

Chapter 11

Continuous Improvement

Continuous improvement, also known as continuous improvement process (CIP) or continuous improvement management (CIM), is a systematic approach to enhancing organizational processes, products, services, and practices over time. It involves ongoing efforts to identify opportunities for improvement, implement changes, monitor results, and make further refinements to achieve higher levels of efficiency, quality, and performance. Continuous improvement is rooted in the philosophy of Kaizen, which emphasizes the pursuit of incremental and sustainable improvements across all areas of an organization. Here are key aspects and principles of continuous improvement for businesses:

Cultural Mindset:

Kaizen Philosophy: Instill a culture of continuous improvement throughout the organization by promoting the Kaizen philosophy, which encourages every employee to contribute ideas, identify problems, and participate in improvement initiatives.

Ownership and Accountability: Foster a sense of ownership and accountability among employees at all levels by empowering them to take ownership of their work processes, identify improvement opportunities, and implement changes to drive positive outcomes.

Iterative Process: Plan Do Check Act (PDCA) Cycle: Adopt the PDCA cycle as a framework for continuous improvement, consisting of four stages: Plan (identify areas for improvement and develop a plan), Do (implement changes on a small scale), Check (evaluate results and gather feedback), Act (make adjustments and standardize improvements).

Iterative Approach: Embrace an iterative approach to improvement, where small, incremental changes are tested, evaluated, and refined over time to drive cumulative progress and sustainable results.

Data Driven Decision-Making:

Performance Metrics: Establish key performance indicators (KPIs) and metrics to measure the effectiveness, efficiency, and quality of processes, products, and services.

Data Collection and Analysis: Collect and analyze relevant data to identify trends, patterns, root causes of problems, and areas of inefficiency or waste. Use data driven insights to prioritize improvement opportunities and guide decision-making.

Employee Engagement: Employee Involvement: Engage employees in improvement initiatives by soliciting their input, ideas, and feedback on how to streamline processes, enhance productivity, and deliver greater value to customers.

Training and Development: Provide training, coaching, and resources to employees to enhance their problem solving skills, creativity, and understanding of continuous improvement principles and techniques.

Cross Functional Collaboration:

Teamwork and Collaboration: Foster collaboration and teamwork across departments, functions, and levels of the organization to address complex challenges and drive holistic improvements that span multiple areas or processes.

Interdisciplinary Approaches: Encourage interdisciplinary approaches to problem solving and improvement, leveraging diverse perspectives, expertise, and skills to generate innovative solutions and drive organizational learning.

Customer Focus:

Voice of the Customer (VOC): Incorporate the voice of the customer into continuous improvement efforts by actively seeking feedback, understanding customer needs and preferences, and aligning improvement initiatives with customer expectations.

Value Stream Mapping: Use value stream mapping techniques to identify and eliminate nonvalue added activities, streamline processes, and deliver greater value to customers by reducing lead times, improving quality, and enhancing responsiveness.

Leadership Support:

Leadership Commitment: Demonstrate visible and active support for continuous improvement initiatives from top leadership, including allocating resources, removing barriers, and fostering a culture of experimentation, learning, and adaptation.

Change Management: Implement effective change management practices to ensure that improvements are effectively communicated, understood, and embraced throughout the organization, minimizing resistance and maximizing adoption.

Continuous improvement is not a onetime project or initiative but rather a mindset and a way of operating that permeates the entire organization. By embracing continuous improvement principles and practices, businesses can adapt to changing market conditions, enhance competitiveness, and drive sustainable growth and success over the long term.

Chapter 11.1
Feedback Mechanisms

The processes and systems put in place to collect, analyze, and act upon feedback from various stakeholders, including customers, employees, suppliers, and partners. These mechanisms enable organizations to gather insights, identify areas for improvement, and make informed decisions to enhance performance, products, services, and processes. Here's an overview of feedback mechanisms in business and factors to consider for their effective implementation:

Types of Feedback Mechanisms:

Customer Feedback:

Surveys: Conduct customer satisfaction surveys, Net Promoter Score (NPS) surveys, or feedback forms to gather feedback on products, services, and overall customer experience.

Feedback Platforms: Utilize online review platforms, social media channels, and customer feedback portals to capture customer comments, reviews, and suggestions.

Customer Support Interactions: Monitor and analyze interactions with customer support teams, including calls, emails, and live chats, to identify recurring issues and customer pain points.

Employee Feedback:

Performance Reviews: Conduct regular performance reviews and feedback sessions between managers and employees to discuss goals, achievements, and areas for development.

Employee Surveys: Administer employee engagement surveys, pulse surveys, or 360degree feedback assessments to gather insights on workplace satisfaction, morale, and organizational culture.

Suggestion Box: Implement a suggestion box or digital platform where employees can anonymously submit suggestions, ideas, and feedback for improvement.

Supplier and Partner Feedback:

Supplier Surveys: Send surveys or questionnaires to suppliers and partners to evaluate their performance, quality of products or services, and collaboration effectiveness.

Partner Meetings: Schedule regular meetings or checkins with key suppliers and partners to discuss collaboration opportunities, challenges, and feedback.

Factors to Consider for Effective Feedback Mechanisms:

Clarity of Purpose: Clearly define the purpose and objectives of feedback mechanisms, ensuring alignment with organizational goals, values, and priorities.

Accessibility and Ease of Use: Make feedback mechanisms accessible and user friendly for stakeholders, utilizing multiple channels and formats to accommodate diverse preferences and needs.

Anonymity and Confidentiality: Offer options for anonymity or confidentiality when soliciting feedback, particularly in sensitive or contentious areas, to encourage honest and candid responses.

Timeliness and Frequency: Collect feedback regularly and in a timely manner to capture real time insights and address issues promptly before they escalate.

Actionable Insights: Design feedback mechanisms to generate actionable insights and recommendations that can inform decision-making, problem solving, and improvement efforts.

Closed Loop Feedback: Establish processes for closing the feedback loop by acknowledging receipt of feedback, providing updates on actions taken in response, and soliciting follow up input from stakeholders.

Feedback Culture: Cultivate a culture that values feedback, encourages open communication, and embraces constructive criticism as opportunities for learning and growth.

Integration with Systems: Integrate feedback mechanisms with existing systems, processes, and workflows to streamline data collection, analysis, and dissemination, minimizing duplication of effort and maximizing efficiency.

Training and Support: Provide training, resources, and support to stakeholders involved in administering, analyzing, and acting upon feedback, ensuring proficiency and consistency in feedback management practices.

Continuous Improvement: Continuously evaluate and refine feedback mechanisms based on lessons learned, stakeholder feedback, and evolving organizational needs and priorities, striving for ongoing improvement and innovation.

By implementing effective feedback mechanisms and considering these factors, businesses can gather valuable insights, strengthen stakeholder relationships, drive organizational improvement, and ultimately enhance performance and competitiveness in the marketplace.

Chapter 11.2

Process Improvement Initiatives

These initiatives refer to systematic efforts aimed at enhancing the efficiency, effectiveness, and quality of organizational processes. These initiatives involve analyzing existing processes, identifying areas for improvement, implementing changes, and monitoring results to achieve better outcomes. Here's an overview of process improvement initiatives in business and factors to consider for their successful implementation:

Types of Process Improvement Initiatives:

Lean Management: Lean principles focus on eliminating waste, streamlining workflows, and optimizing processes to maximize value delivery to customers while minimizing resources, time, and costs.

Six Sigma: Six Sigma methodologies aim to reduce variation and defects in processes by using statistical tools and techniques to measure, analyze, and improve process performance.

Business Process Reengineering (BPR): BPR involves redesigning and restructuring processes from the ground up to achieve radical improvements in performance, often leveraging technology and automation.

Continuous Improvement (Kaizen): Kaizen emphasizes continuous, incremental improvements in processes, products, and services through small, incremental changes driven by employee involvement and empowerment.

Total Quality Management (TQM): TQM focuses on continuous quality improvement across all aspects of the organization, emphasizing customer satisfaction, employee involvement, and process excellence.

Factors to Consider for Process Improvement Initiatives:

Clear Objectives: Define clear objectives and goals for process improvement initiatives, aligning them with strategic priorities, customer needs, and organizational values.

Stakeholder Engagement: Involve stakeholders, including employees, customers, suppliers, and partners, in the process improvement efforts to gain diverse perspectives, insights, and buy in.

Data Driven Analysis: Collect and analyze data to identify bottlenecks, inefficiencies, and opportunities for improvement within processes. Use key performance indicators (KPIs), metrics, and benchmarking to measure process performance and progress.

Root Cause Analysis: Conduct root cause analysis to identify underlying causes of problems or issues within processes, enabling targeted interventions and solutions.

Cross Functional Collaboration: Foster collaboration and communication across departments, teams, and functions to address process improvement initiatives that span organizational boundaries.

Continuous Monitoring and Review: Establish mechanisms for ongoing monitoring, review, and evaluation of process performance to ensure sustained improvement and identify new opportunities for optimization.

Change Management: Implement effective change management practices to manage resistance, communicate effectively, and ensure successful adoption of process improvements across the organization.

Technology and Automation: Leverage technology and automation tools to streamline processes, eliminate manual tasks, and enhance efficiency and scalability.

Training and Skill Development: Provide training, education, and skill development opportunities to employees to equip them with the knowledge, skills, and tools needed to support process improvement efforts.

Leadership Support and Commitment: Secure leadership support and commitment for process improvement initiatives, including allocating resources, removing barriers, and championing a culture of continuous improvement.

Customer Focus: Keep the customer at the center of process improvement initiatives, prioritizing improvements that enhance customer experience, satisfaction, and value delivery.

Sustainability and Scalability: Ensure that process improvements are sustainable over the long term and scalable to accommodate future growth, changes, and evolving business needs.

By considering these factors and implementing systematic process improvement initiatives, businesses can drive operational excellence, enhance competitiveness, and deliver greater value to customers, stakeholders, and the organization as a whole.

Chapter 11.3

Lessons Learned and Best Practices

Lessons learned and best practices in business refer to insights gained from past experiences, successes, and failures, as well as proven methods and approaches that have been identified as effective in achieving desired outcomes. These lessons and practices serve as valuable knowledge assets that organizations can leverage to inform decision-making, improve performance, and drive continuous improvement. Here's an overview of lessons learned, best practices, and factors to consider for their effective application in business:

Lessons Learned:

Lessons learned are insights, conclusions, or recommendations derived from analyzing past experiences, projects, or initiatives. They involve reflecting on what worked well, what didn't, and what could be improved to inform future actions and decisions.

Sources of Lessons Learned:

Project Post Mortems: Conducting post project reviews to evaluate project outcomes, identify successes, challenges, and lessons learned.

Incident and Issue Analysis: Analyzing incidents, errors, or failures to identify root causes, corrective actions, and preventive measures.

Customer Feedback: Incorporating feedback from customers, clients, and stakeholders to understand their experiences, preferences, and expectations.

Industry Benchmarks: Benchmarking against industry standards, competitors, or best practices to identify areas for improvement and opportunities for innovation.

Employee Feedback: Soliciting input and insights from employees at all levels of the organization on process improvements, organizational culture, and leadership effectiveness.

Factors to Consider:

Documentation: Document lessons learned in a structured format, including key findings, recommendations, and action items, to ensure retention and accessibility for future reference.

Analysis and Reflection: Conduct thorough analysis and reflection on lessons learned, considering both positive and negative experiences, to extract meaningful insights and actionable recommendations.

Actionable Recommendations: Generate actionable recommendations and strategies based on lessons learned to inform decision-making, problem solving, and improvement efforts.

Communication and Sharing: Communicate lessons learned effectively across the organization, ensuring that relevant stakeholders have access to valuable insights and knowledge.

Continuous Learning Culture: Foster a culture of continuous learning, curiosity, and openness to feedback, where employees are encouraged to reflect on experiences and share insights for collective learning and improvement.

Implementation and Follow Up

Implement lessons learned into practice by incorporating them into organizational processes, policies, and procedures. Follow up regularly to assess the effectiveness of implemented recommendations and iterate as needed.

Best Practices:

Best practices are established methods, techniques, or approaches that have been identified as effective and efficient in achieving specific goals or outcomes. They represent proven strategies or principles that have been validated through experience and research.

Types of Best Practices:

Operational Best Practices: Standard operating procedures, processes, or techniques that have been refined over time to optimize efficiency, quality, and performance.

Industry Best Practices: Practices or standards recognized and adopted by leading organizations within a particular industry or sector as benchmarks for excellence.

Functional Best Practices: Practices specific to functional areas such as marketing, finance, human resources, or supply chain management, which have been shown to drive superior results.

Cross Functional Best Practices: Practices that cut across multiple departments or functions, addressing complex challenges or opportunities that require collaboration and coordination.

Factors to Consider:

Relevance: Assess the relevance and applicability of best practices to the organization's goals, context, and specific challenges or opportunities.

Adaptation: Tailor best practices to fit the organization's unique needs, culture, and operating environment, rather than adopting them blindly.

Continuous Improvement: Continuously evaluate and refine best practices based on changing conditions, emerging trends, and lessons learned from implementation.

Benchmarking: Benchmark against industry peers, competitors, or leading organizations to identify and adopt best practices that drive superior performance and outcomes.

Training and Education: Provide training, education, and resources to employees on best practices, ensuring widespread understanding and adoption across the organization.

Measurement and Evaluation: Establish metrics, KPIs, or performance indicators to measure the effectiveness and impact of best practices on organizational performance and outcomes.

By leveraging lessons learned and adopting best practices, businesses can enhance decision-making, mitigate risks, improve efficiency, and drive sustainable growth and success. It's essential to systematically capture, analyze, and apply insights from past experiences and industry knowledge to continuously improve and innovate in today's dynamic business environment.

Conclusion

In conclusion, a business playbook serves as a comprehensive guide and reference document that outlines key strategies, processes, policies, and best practices for operating and managing a business effectively. It provides a structured framework for decision-making, problem solving, and execution, enabling consistency, alignment, and accountability across the organization. The importance of a business playbook lies in its ability to:

Facilitate Alignment

By clearly defining the company's mission, vision, values, objectives, and strategies, a playbook ensures that all stakeholders are aligned and working towards common goals.

Drive Consistency

Standardized processes, procedures, and guidelines outlined in the playbook promote consistency in operations, decision-making, and customer experiences, regardless of changes in personnel or circumstances.

Enhance Efficiency: Streamlined workflows, documented best practices, and clear roles and responsibilities outlined in the playbook contribute to operational efficiency, productivity, and resource optimization.

Mitigate Risks: Policies, protocols, and contingency plans included in the playbook help identify and mitigate risks, ensuring business continuity and resilience in the face of challenges or disruptions.

Support Growth and Scalability: A scalable playbook provides a foundation for growth by enabling the organization to replicate successful strategies, adapt to changing market conditions, and onboard new employees efficiently.

Promote Learning and Development: By capturing lessons learned, best practices, and performance metrics, a playbook fosters a culture of continuous learning, improvement, and innovation within the organization.

Overall, a well designed and regularly updated business playbook serves as a valuable tool for guiding strategic decision-making, promoting operational excellence, and driving sustainable growth and success in today's dynamic business landscape. It empowers organizations to navigate challenges, capitalize on opportunities, and deliver exceptional value to customers, employees, and stakeholders.

Commitment to Excellence Pledge

Commitment to Excellence As we embark on this journey of utilizing our business playbook to drive success and excellence, let us make the following commitment:

Commitment to Excellence Pledge

An example to allow for you to create your own.

At [Company Name], we are committed to excellence in all aspects of our business. With the implementation of our comprehensive business playbook, we pledge to uphold the highest standards of quality, innovation, and customer satisfaction. Here's our commitment:

Delivering Value: We will continuously strive to deliver exceptional value to our customers by understanding their needs, exceeding their expectations, and providing products and services of unparalleled quality and reliability.

Continuous Improvement: We will embrace a culture of continuous improvement, leveraging insights from our playbook to identify opportunities for enhancement, streamline processes, and drive innovation across our organization.

Operational Excellence: We will maintain operational excellence by adhering to standardized processes, optimizing efficiencies, and fostering a culture of accountability, collaboration, and transparency within our teams.

Customer Centric Approach: We will prioritize the needs and preferences of our customers in every decision we make, leveraging the insights and feedback captured in our playbook to tailor our offerings and experiences to their evolving requirements.

Empowering Our Team: We will empower our team members with the knowledge, resources, and support they need to excel in their roles, fostering a culture of learning, growth, and empowerment that drives individual and organizational success.

Adaptability and Resilience: We will remain agile, adaptable, and resilient in the face of challenges and uncertainties, leveraging the guidance and strategies outlined in our playbook to navigate obstacles and seize opportunities for growth and advancement.

Ethical Conduct: We will conduct our business with the utmost integrity, honesty, and ethical conduct, adhering to the principles and values outlined in our playbook and upholding the trust and confidence of our customers, partners, and stakeholders.

Measurable Results: We will measure our progress, track our performance against key metrics and benchmarks, and hold ourselves accountable for achieving the goals and objectives outlined in our playbook.

Sharing Knowledge and Insights: We will actively share knowledge, insights, and best practices captured in our playbook with our team members, fostering collaboration, learning, and continuous improvement across our organization.

Striving for Excellence: We will not settle for mediocrity or complacency. Instead, we will continuously push the boundaries of what's possible, striving for excellence in everything we do and setting new standards of success for ourselves and our industry.

With this commitment to excellence and the guidance of our business playbook, we are poised to achieve remarkable results, exceed expectations, and create a future filled with growth, prosperity, and lasting impact. Let us embark on this journey together, united in our pursuit of excellence and unwavering in our dedication to success.

Call to Action

To all businesses striving for success and sustainability, the adoption of a comprehensive business playbook is not just a recommendation; it's an imperative step towards achieving your goals.

Bring your company or your idea of company to fruition and adopt a business playbook for your own . By utilizing the playbook and allowing it to guide you. Your company can

- Unlock Your Full Potential: Transform your business operations from reactive to proactive by implementing a structured playbook that guides every aspect of your organization.
- Navigate Challenges with Confidence: Equip your team with the tools, strategies, and best practices they need to tackle challenges headon, ensuring resilience and adaptability in a rapidly changing market.
- Drive Sustainable Growth: Lay the foundation for scalable growth and expansion by establishing standardized processes, streamlining workflows, and optimizing resource allocation.
- Harness Collective Wisdom: Tap into the collective wisdom of your team and industry experts by capturing lessons learned, best practices, and innovative solutions within your playbook.
- Foster Collaboration and Alignment: Foster a culture of collaboration, alignment, and accountability across your organization, ensuring that everyone is working towards a shared vision and common goals.
- Safeguard Your Future: Mitigate risks, enhance operational efficiency, and safeguard business continuity by implementing robust policies, protocols, and contingency plans outlined in your playbook.
- Commit to Continuous Improvement: Embrace a mindset of continuous improvement and innovation by regularly updating and refining your playbook based on evolving market dynamics, customer feedback, and lessons learned.

- Set Yourself Apart: Stand out in your industry as a forward thinking, agile, and customer centric organization that is committed to excellence and delivering exceptional value.
- Take Action Today: Don't wait for tomorrow to start reaping the benefits of a business playbook. Take action now to empower your business, inspire your team, and unlock a brighter future filled with growth and success

Remember, your business playbook isn't just a document; it's your roadmap to success. Embrace it, implement it, and watch your business thrive like never before.

Reach out to STRIVE Coaching Inc today to assist you in this powerful journey. https//:s-t-r-i-v-e.com

www.ingramcontent.com/pod-product-compliance
Lightning Source LLC
Chambersburg PA
CBHW071211240526
45470CB00018B/1707